You Don't Own Money

YOU DON'T OWN MONEY

▼

But It Can Own You

Roger A. Sorensen

Writers Club Press
San Jose New York Lincoln Shanghai

You Don't Own Money
But It Can Own You

Writers Club Press
an imprint of iUniverse.com, Inc.

For information address:
iUniverse.com, Inc.
5220 S 16th, Ste. 200
Lincoln, NE 68512
www.iuniverse.com

ISBN: 0-595-18681-5

Printed in the United States of America

CONTENTS

LISTING OF CHARTS AND SAMPLES

ACKNOWLEDGEMENTS

I would like to take a second here and acknowledge the intelligent and wonderful people who have been working in the Financial Education business for many years. Many hours have been spent listening to what they have to say, reading what they labored to write, and absorbing their teachings. But please, don't get me wrong. While I admire what the following people have done, this book is my own work and so bears no reflection on any of them.

I especially want to thank Larry Burkett, Ron Blue, and Terry Spencer for their wonderful ideas and writings.

And of course who can forget my lovely wife Jennifer. Thank you for the continuous support and tutoring me in the proper use of the English Language these past many months.

PROLOGUE–
AN INTRODUCTION

Let me start this off by thanking you for picking this book up and actually opening it to the beginning. Far too many people who think they want to learn about managing their finances are in a hurry and so skip to the chapter that sounds like the one they want. That is not the proper method of doing things.

Just as reading this book for the first time requires effort and an investment of time on your part, so too does financial management take effort and patience to obtain a usable level of knowledge.

As you read the words I've set down on paper you'll likely notice that I am not a strict by-the-rule writer. I think after a page or two you will most likely get the rhythm of my rambling words. I tend to think twice as fast as my fingers move so the words are always playing catch-up. This has the tendency to create a conversation type of writing style. If I would put a comma behind a word when I talk, that is often where I will put a comma when I type.

I have strived to create an engaging (I won't say fun), interest holding and yet informative book about basic finances. There are countless books by countless authors on the subject of investing. You can even find an Investing for Dummies, just like those DOS for Dummies books of years gone by. But it would appear that a shortage of financial education books exists.

After all, what difference does it make if a book tells you how to invest $100 a month in the stock market when creditors are harassing you about your late car payment? Don't get me wrong, those investment books are wonderful (if you get the right one). However, a person really does need to have a solid financial base upon which to build their investment portfolio before they strive to reach the stars.

This book covers the basics of financial management including – setting goals, developing a financial plan, how to take your financial plan and smash it into a budget, and some practical tips (albeit not very many) about making it easier to get a budget working for you.

It does not cover investments, how to pay off debt (I mention debt, though I wrote this book assuming you would have little or no consumer debt), nor does this book cover how to minimize taxes.

All in all, I trust you will enjoy reading this book and perhaps you will even find something useful within these pages you will be able to apply towards your own financial life.

PROLOGUE ENCORE–
I AM NOT READY YET

Why, you have probably asked yourself more than once, did I give this book the title I did?

The answer is…

It is the truth.

Benjamin Franklin has a quote (one of many) of which I enjoy. He says, "The use of money is all the advantage there is in having it."

You can own a car, a house, or even a chair. Why in this modern day there are a few people who actually claim to own a CAT!

But you cannot own money because money is nothing more than an accepted physical representation of wealth. Paper money in and of itself has no real value. And that is what people think of today when you talk money. Paper and ink—nothing more, and nothing less – with the sole purpose of representing the transfer of wealth from one person to another.

Later in the book, somewhere in the first chapter to be more exact, you will find the three requirements of money to be accepted as money. So the more you think about the concept of money, the more you will be likely to recognize it is almost an ideal, an accepted belief that will survive only so long as two or more people say it will survive.

So unlike a physical chair that can stand on its own two legs (four if you insist), money is not something you can own.

CHAPTER ONE –
ECONOMIC INFORMATION

Let's start this financial primer with the basics. We'll get into what an economy is, how the current United States economy began and more in a little while. But for now we can break all the information and mis-information down into a single base question.

WHAT DOES MONEY MEAN TO YOU?!

To many people it could be that money means security. To others it means accomplishment. But what does it mean to you? Does the absence of money mean that you are a failure? I would certainly hope money means none of the above. All to often people hold the wrong attitude about money because of what we believe money can do for us. Society tells us money can do all and be all to us even though it has a multitude of limitations.

Benjamin Franklin once said, "The use of money is all the advantage there is in having it."

Go back and reread that line. I'll wait.

And yes, I do realize I quoted that line in the second prologue. So what? I like it.

Having money does not mean you have anything until you spend it. We've all heard the old wish for 'All the money in the world'. But why?

If you had every item anyone has ever called money, you have to spend it to eat. Once you spend it, you no longer have all the money in the world. You can own the item that forms money, but until you spend it you have no advantage over those who don't have money. Even when you do spend it, there are many things money cannot do.

Money cannot guarantee freedom to do whatever you want. Even Donald Trump cannot drive fifty miles per hour in a fifteen mph zone without running the risk of a ticket. Laws will always exist that curb our freedoms, even if you controlled all the money in the world.

Money may allow you to buy just about anything you want, but think about that one for a moment. If you could have anything you desire how long would it be before possessions give you little pleasure? Often many times it is the hunt – the saving, the scrimping and working hard for what we want – that gives us weeks of enjoyment while we anticipate, we plan, and we dream. Then the actual capture – the purchase – holds little more than a few moments pleasure before we are hunting for the next purchase.

It is my personal belief that this is why some people are shopoholics. They enjoy the rush of searching out and finding something to buy. That's the shopping part. But once they have bought the thing they got the rush from looking for, the thrill is over. So they have to buy something else to reattain that rush.

Let's look at that old myth that goes something like this: If you are successful you will earn a large salary, and if you earn a large salary you will be happy. Sound about right?

Success and happiness are not bought with money nor do they come with the things money can buy. There is no correlation between wealth and happiness. When a person has all the money they need, the resulting accumulation of possessions in pursuit of happiness can push them to the edge of not having enough money to live; they are so busy paying for every latest and greatest item they think will make them happy they don't hear the knock of real happiness at their door.

Read about these nine men who had more than enough money to qualify as successful and thus happy – according to the thinking of society anyway. Some of these names you might recognize even though the first list is from 1923. If you have seen this list before then kudos to you; but if this is your first time reading it than remember them well for in their day they had it all – money, fame, power and high position.

1. Arthur Cotton – a great wheat speculator
2. Albert Fall – the Secretary of the Interior for President Harding
3. Leon Fraser – president of Bank of International Settlements
4. Howard Hopson – president of the largest gas company
5. Samuel Insull – president of the largest electric utility company
6. Ivar Kreuger – head of the world's greatest monopoly
7. Jesse Livermore – Wall Streets greatest 'bear'
8. Charles Schwab – president of the largest steel company
9. Richard Whitney – president of the New York Stock Exchange

While these men made great fortunes, their lives were anything but happy or successful. If they had been happy or successful what do you suppose their lives would be like by the time this second list? This list is from 1948 and shows the result of their lives.

1. Arthur Cotton – died abroad and broke
2. Albert Fall – pardoned so he could die at home and abroad
3. Leon Fraser – died by his own hand
4. Howard Hopson – was mentally insane
5. Samuel Insull – died a fugitive abroad and broke
6. Ivar Kreuger – died by his own hand

7.   Jesse Livermore – died by his own hand
8.   Charles Schwab – lived the last five years of his life on bor-
       rowed money
9.   Richard Whitney – was released from Sing Sing prison

Not a very happy list is it.

If someone could have asked these men in 1923 if they were content, more than likely they all would have said yes. But to be content one
cannot depend on money. Mr. Webster says that contentment means,
"satisfied, ease-of-mind". True contentment does not rely on outside influ-
ences such as money for satisfaction.

According to that definition these men were anything but content. And most likely they were not very happy either. To add insult to
injury, I would not call any of them successful either. Suicide, broke, a
fugitive from justice are not signs of successful people in my book.

With that having been said and a few of the dangers of money
hinted at and pointed out to you, let's examine how money came into
being as an item supposedly that has value.

Money is defined in the Merriam Webster Dictionary as "something accepted as a medium of exchange". In other words, money is simply nothing more than a means of facilitating the transfer of wealth. As
either metal or paper it is an arbitrary symbol accepted by the people in a
society to move wealth from the buyer to the seller (thus the exchange).

Maybe we should step back a little further from the money question and ask just 'What is wealth if money transfers it from one person to
another?'

The answer is not all that clear. The Merriam Webster Dictionary
says Wealth is "an abundance of material possessions" and Wealthy as
"rich". Rich is even more subjective in stating that essentially you are Rich
if you "control great wealth".

In that case, many people today could say someone earning $100,000 a year is Rich. But someone from a poverty-stricken Central American nation might say someone earning $1000 a year is Rich. Defining monetary values is very subjective, no matter how hard so called experts work to prove their thoughts and definitions are perfectly objective and not subject to interpretation.

Civilizations in the distant past often based their calculations of wealth on a family's number of cattle or camel's, the acres of land they possessed, or some other means of accounting. On one South Pacific Island the size and number of wheel stones a man owns measures his wealth. Since these can be over six feet in diameter these wheels of wealth are anything but pocket change!

One of the wealthiest families from that South Pacific Island have not seen their money wheel for at least two generations. The wheel was being transported by canoe when a sudden wave swamped the canoe and the wheel sank to the ocean floor. The stone is still considered to have value by the islanders, even though they can not see or move the wheel, because their grandfathers told of seeing that great money wheel.

In the United States prior to the Industrial Revolution wealth was measured by land ownership or the amount of controlled natural resources such as gold and silver mines. Starting in the years after the American War Between the States, currency became the accepted measure of wealth. More specifically, the more possessions one could buy with their currency, the 'wealthier' society considered them to be.

Thus we arrive at today where currency is a term nearly always reserved for use at financial institutions and money is what those of us in the general public spends. But how did we reach the point of bartering our 'money' for goods and services and all the items we buy every day?

To use an old example lets look at Charles who raises cows, George who raises grain and Bob who is a blacksmith manufacturing horseshoes and nails. Now that the background is set, here's the story of our economy – the barter of money for goods.

HOW MONEY CAME TO BE
BARTERED FOR GOODS

Charles decides to build a barn with lumber he has cut from his own property and allowed to air-dry. Instead of using pegs to hold the boards together he wants nails. He goes to Bob.

Charles–"Bob, I'll trade you a cow for ten pounds of nails."
Bob–"Sounds good to me, Charles."

That went so well, Charles decides he needs more nails for his next project. But there is a problem. Bob doesn't need more than one cow!

Bob–"Sorry Charlie. One cow is all that I need."
Charles–"George, how about I trade my cow for your corn?
George–"I could use a cow. Let's trade.
Charles–"Okay, Bob. I've got some corn I can trade you for nails."
Bob–"Sounds good to me."

So Charles has what he wants, George has what he wants, and Bob has what he wants. Everyone is happy. Then people other than just Charles, George and Bob latch onto this idea of trading items for nails. Not only did people trade stuff for Bob's nails, they started trading amongst themselves for nails.

In the above scenario, nails have become acceptable to the people as 'money'. This is a simple example of local economic development in a region. George, Bob, and Charles have shown what the term economic means – "the production, development and management of material wealth".

Bob creates the material wealth in the form of nails. These nails are 'spent' by Charles and George to acquire the items they desire.

Let's take the scenario one step further so it more closely resembles our economy by introducing a new medium of exchange. Paper Money!

Bob – "Here's your nails, George."

George – "I'd like you to keep the nails and give me a piece of paper saying

I have them stored here. Okay?"

Bob – "Can do. I'll just keep them out here in my warehouse."

George has discovered how much simpler it is to carry around paper than a bunch of nails to make his purchases. There is nothing wrong with paper money like this because the nails stored at Bob's is securing the paper money.

Before people will accept an item – whether nails, gold, or seashells – as money, that item must satisfy three important functions.

1. Money must have value to the people in the economy.
2. Money must be storable by the people who have the item.
3. Money must be capable of being divided and not losing its value.

At first nails satisfied all three functions and so were accepted as money in the region around Bob's blacksmith shop where he made nails. Then, when he began issuing paper money that could be redeemed for nails stored in his warehouse, the paper money was accepted as meeting the same functions as the nails. So both nails and the paper money were acceptable as money to the people.

Are we together on this so far? The development of nails as money is comparable to what has happened for most of mankind's economic history. Only the money was not in the form of nails but gold or silver coins. Usually with the likeness of a countries ruler stamped on the coins face.

In the United States, paper money has long been issued in small quantities by the federal government and other institutions—including banks! Those institutions that survived the economic disasters and upheavals of the first 150+ years of the countries life did so with paper money backed by gold or silver _on demand_. Gold and silver of course are nothing special in and of themselves except for the fact that neither is in great supply and both have long been accepted as mediums of exchange.

So Bob's nails stored in his warehouse act like the gold in Fort Knox. Because the money of the United States was redeemable for gold or silver on demand, it was considered secure and accepted around the world without hesitation. This remained true until August 1971 when then-President "I am not a crook" Nixon took the United States off the gold standard – essentially telling the world our money was guaranteed to be worth only the paper it was printed on.

So how smart was the usage of that bit of presidential power?

What affect could this action produce? Unless the government controls its spending, gets out of debt (which it is currently talking about doing), and puts this country back on a sound financial foundation there is only one possible result. This is the same result that would happen if a business tried to spend its way to prosperity without worrying about how to pay back its creditors. BANKRUPTCY!!

Do I think the United States government will go bankrupt? Not seriously, but right now the government is so intertwined with the national economy that the way the U.S. government goes, so goes the country.

PROBLEMS IN THE KINGDOM OF
NAILS

Consider Bob and the nail secured economy that is flourishing around his shop.

Charles – "Bob, I need some nails but I can't pay for them until next Tuesday."
Bob – "No problem. I'll loan you nails from my warehouse."

Now that Bob is making loans of nails in his warehouse, he has metamorphosed into a banker. Bob did not create new nails to loan out to Charles, instead he loaned out nails deposited (stored) in his warehouse that belonged to someone else.

Unlike before when Bob created paper money that met the same three functions as the nail money this time Bob created 'funny money'. Another name for funny money is 'credit'.

Credit comes from the Latin term *credere* – meaning, "to believe". As long as George and Charles and the other depositors believe Bob can satisfy them if they demand to redeem their paper money for nails, Bob will stay in business.

Although credit looks like money, acts like money and quacks like money, it is not money. It is storable, and divisible to the people but it contains no value. When Bob made nails and stored them for his customers he made something to back the paper money issued. When he issues a piece of paper on nails in storage that belong to someone else, he is expending no effort or cost to make the money. It is worth only the paper it is printed on.

So what happens when people fail to continue their belief in Bob and his bank? Let's look and learn.

George – "I'm here to redeem my paper money for nails, Bob."

Bob – "I can do that tomorrow, George. I only have half enough nails for you."

George – "Tomorrow? This paper says 'on demand'! Not tomorrow."

Charles – "Say Bob, I want to redeem this paper today for nails as well."

Bob – "I can't do it today. I need until tomorrow."

The people in the area are suddenly aware of what Bob has done. A run begins on his supply of nails in the warehouse with depositors suddenly wanting their money (nails) back from him. And he is caught without enough nails to satisfy them all.

Do you suppose that if Bob did not have enough nails to cover the paper money you wanted to redeem that you would be happy if he issued you a credit slip promising to pay tomorrow? I doubt it. You already have a credit slip in your hand.

Our belief in Bob's ability to pay is gone. Suddenly the only things that will make all the people happy are cold hard nails. They want their money back and Bob is caught short. He is forced to close his doors and declare himself bankrupt. Or in this case he is nailrupt.

What happens to the people who failed to get their paper money redeemed for nails before Bob closed? They're out of luck and left holding paper money worth only the value of the paper itself. If they have bills to pay and don't have enough nails to pay with, then they too are bankrupt. After all, if Bob is closed than what value does a piece of paper good for nails stored at Bob's hold?

When the belief in credit money (funny money) shatters against the blunt edge of financial reality entire economies fall apart leaving nothing of value behind.

CHAPTER TWO–
CREDIT EQUALS DEBT

We've seen how credit imitates money but it lacks one of the three important functions of money. Credit holds no value to the people in the economy. At the same time when you purchase an item on credit you are creating something of value to the lending company – DEBT.

The only reason this debt can be said to have value for the lending institution is because you have to pay interest on the outstanding balance of the credit they have lent to you. No matter what anyone says to the contrary there is no way to avoid the fact that "Credit equals Debt".

CREDIT HISTORY (no, not yours)

Until the past 50 years, every economy in the history of mankind has relied on money as mediums of exchange. This money had to hold the three functions people in the economy required – to have Value, to be Storable, and to be Divisible. If a buyer did not have the accepted money, they did not get the goods. No cash, no purchase was the motto of the day.

Occasionally a storekeeper would extend a line of credit to an individual or his family. But that was fairly rare because if the buyer failed to pay, the storekeeper was out of his ability to pay for the goods he'd given away. So if a line of credit was extended, the storekeeper was confident of the buyers' ability to repay in a few weeks at most.

Credit is a privilege for consumers; it is not a right.

As I mentioned, it is only in the last 50 years that credit has become the money of choice for people to make their purchases. The current attitude towards consumer debt began shortly after World War II. During the war the government had dug itself deeply into debt trying to supply the military with ammunition, the people at home with just enough products to keep morale up and much of this was funded with borrowing called war bonds. Bonds are a fancy way of saying debt.

With the war won and the GI's coming home there became a demand for housing. By 1955 98% of all new housing starts were funded by lending institutions. A short thirty years before during another construction boom (1928) the exact opposite happened. A mere 2% of new construction was paid for with debt.

FIGURES NEVER LIE BUT LIARS FIG-URE

While on the subject of statistics, this is as good of place as any to insert a few more to demonstrate how the idea of spending funny money has caught on in the United States.

1.   In 1978 $45 billion more was added to consumer debt than was paid off.
2.   In 1980 $303 billion was owed on credit cards, car loans, and personal loans.
3.   By 1992 consumer debt (including credit cards, auto and personal loans) reached $720 billion.
4.   This means the average family pays over 20 cents of every after-tax dollar just to make payments on consumer debt.
5.   When you add in mortgage debt, auto debt, personal debt to credit card debt by the late 1990's the average family owed 1.5 times its annual income.

If you could ask every divorced couple what was the number one problem that put their marriage on a course of disaster you would find that nearly 70% would reply "money". And what is credit but funny money – money without value? The lack of cash money was not the real source of arguments for these couples, nor was it the over abundance of money. They fought about the consumer debt that was demanding more and more of their cash.

The movies portray the people of the Depression years (the 1930's) as being dirt poor and barely making ends meet. They lived in cramped housing with dirty wood floors and wore second hand clothing that was always grungy. Yet almost none of these people owed a dime to someone else.

Now take a look at the typical family of today. The house is larger with wall-to-wall carpet; the clothing is clean thanks to a new washing machine/dryer matching set. But has the financial situation really changed all that much? You bet it has and you'll agree when you look back at the statistics and see that the average family owes 150% of its annual income to some lender.

Recently I heard a statistic announcing that the typical family earning under $75000 a year had less than $10000 in assets that could be converted to cash – excluding their house.

$75000 is the cut off point because those who will make class distinctions in the United States have declared that anyone earning more than $75000 annually is a high-income earner. I suppose when nearly 50% of the nations wage earners receive $25000 or less that $75000 a year looks like a high income. But we all have to have something to aspire to, don't we?

How much more would those earning less than $75000 each and every year have to add to their assets if credit is not debt? Remember, all debt comes with a price and that price is interest.

ENJOY THE ADVERTISEMENTS – JUST DON'T BUY THE GOODS

Lets take a look around you at all the advertisements for consumer goods. The big chain stores selling furniture or appliances. Even the carpet and wall covering stores are running the same advertisements. "Buy now and no payments for six months! (Or twelve, twenty four, pick a month any month)."

We've all seen them and they all sound so good they must be working in my favor. Get a clue – THEY'RE NOT IN YOUR FAVOR!

Lets look at a simple purchase at one of these stores where you make no payments and pay no interest for twelve long months. First of all, you'll be surprised at how quickly those twelve months go by and if you are like most people, you still have somehow managed to not get the cash together to pay off that loan. Worse, your furniture is now a year old and is starting to show its wear and you still owe 100% on it, plus interest.

Now, back to the original purchase scenario. You enter the store to buy a new easy chair – one of those comfortable recliner styles. It costs only $299 but the salesman is kind enough to point out that if you buy $399 worth of items you don't have to pay a single solitary hot little red penny for anything you take home for a full year. Wow! So you go ahead and buy that new couch you've been thinking about but didn't have the cash for just yet. Now you owe $799 to the store but wait a minute. Here's a lamp, and a new area rug and another chair and this and that and…and…and…

Do you get the picture of why credit can be dangerous? You go into a store willing to pay $299 in cash and come out with the $299 and owing $1500. But that's not so bad you say. That $1500 is not due for twelve months. That's only $125 each month and you've got it paid for— not to mention having earned 5% interest on it during that time.

Maybe you do, but if you are like most people in this society of ours that $125 is terribly difficult to come up with each and every month. Currently the typical savings rate across the nation is about a –4%. No I did not make a typo—on average the average family earning $25000 or less experiences 4% more money outgo than inflow to the family coffers during the year. You can be sure that is not counterfeit cash being printed in the back yard. It is in the form of charges on credit cards or through stores advertising no payment and no interest.

Our little scenario with you owing $1500 can be carried out to its logical ends. The typical family will not be able to pay the entire $1500 off at the end of the year. So the company extending the credit – no, not the furniture store but the financial institution backing the sales promotion – kindly lets you take 36 months to pay off the balance. Of course they will have to add in the twelve months interest already accumulated and you had read the fine print so you realized that interest would be 15% annually – right? Now you owe $1725 accumulation interest compounded monthly at the rate of 1.25% on the unpaid balance.

You can comfort yourself once this sinks into your head by telling yourself if you had paid this off before the end of the first year it would have cost you $125 each month. Now the principle is only $48 a month and with interest you only have to pay $48.60. That's not so bad, is it? Haven't you just saved yourself $76.40 a month?

I think if you have stayed with this rambling account so far, you already know the answer is no, you have not saved anything. Worse is the fact that now you will be paying for your furniture until it is 4 years old and instead of costing you a mere $1500 now it costs $1750. You've actually lost $62.50 a year in interest. That might not seem like much but how many trips to McDonalds would that be? Or how about treating yourself to a nice night at the local Super 6 Motel? Once a year for four years you could have experienced a mini-vacation.

So the true cost of money includes not only having to finish making payments on four-year-old furniture, you have lost out on buying the other things the interest could have purchased.

No matter how you look at it, credit equals debt. A friend of yours might say they have a credit card with a $10000 line of credit. Don't hurt yourself rushing to tell this friend that what they are holding is a $10000 line of debt. The credit does not exist until the funny money is spent and most likely they'll laugh you off anyway. Once spent the credit become debt and when it begins to bite, they'll know there's a problem.

Of course they will most likely not come to you and admit your wisdom.

Or you might be one of those people who would laugh off a friend attempting to tell you that your oh-so-cool status symbol designer credit card is in reality a dangerous snake of debt waiting to bite when you least expect. In that case you are most likely wondering just what the big deal about debt is? In the 1980's vast fortunes were made on debt. To that I respond with a resounding – and your point is? Those fortunes are mostly gone with the wind and the fortune builder has just been released from a federal penitentiary system.

DEBT ISSUES

One of the biggest problems with debt in general is the fact that the debt is not the real problem but is instead a symptom of the real problem. Please note I am talking only about consumer debt, which in my books can also include credit cards.

Just like a cough can be a symptom of tuberculosis, so is the debt a symptom of the real problem. In most cases of consumer debt the issue is really about – greed, fear, self-indulgence, impatience, lack of self-worth, lack of self-discipline and possibly an entire host of others.

As I said in the paragraphs above, I am taking issue with consumer debt, which also includes credit card debt. The other kinds of debt that may or may not – depending on the circumstances – be legitimate include (1) business debt, (2) investment debt and (3) mortgage debt. These debts can also be a reflection of a problematic issue such as listed earlier. But if the borrower is serious about what the business, the investment or the home these kinds of debts are not a symptom nor a problem but rather a cost of existence. The one notation that must be made about these debts is the borrower must be sure the debt will cash flow before taking it on, otherwise he could just as well be getting a consumer loan.

Anytime debt is taken on four questions need to be asked.

1.   Do the economics of this debt make sense?
2.   Is my spouse in 100% agreement about acquiring this debt?
3.   Do we have the peace of mind and spirit necessary to get this debt?
4.   What goals will this debt meet that cannot be done in any other manner?

Earlier we have discussed the economic dangers of debt. You must pay interest on the debt and thus loose the ability to spend that money on what you want. One item I failed to mention was income tax.

You will have to pay income tax on your income before being able to pay your interest charges. Thus if the total interest on that $1500 debt will be a total of $250 you will need to earn at least $300 (if your tax bracket is 15%). The economic truth is that the $1500 worth if consumer debt is going to cost you at least $1800. So truth be told, by borrowing $1500 to pay for furniture you are admitting at the very least that...

1.   you are impatient and have to have the stuff now
2.   greedy enough to spend tomorrows money today
3.   you lack the self discipline to save until you could pay cash

If the truth hurts, get over it. Don't make purchases like this under any circumstance no matter how good it sounds or how tempting the merchandise looks. Check out the alternative facts.

Had you taken the $48 a month and put it into a savings account earning 5% interest it would have taken you almost 28 months to save $1350. Let's look at this closer.

Why $48 a month – that is how much you ended up paying for three years to the lender. Good enough, now why 28 months – do the math and you'll see you will have almost an even $1350 in the account at the end of that time.

Why $1350 and not the full $1500 the furniture costs? It has been my experience that if you carry cash into those stores offering the kinds of credit terms discussed in this chapter you will find a salesperson willing to cut at least 10% off the cost of the items.

Why would they do this, you really have to ask? The store will not have to complete all the paperwork required by the lender before you are approved for the purchase. The sale is guaranteed; you won't change your mind while waiting in line for approval of the debt. One more big reason stores are willing to deal if you have cash is the fact that part of their sales price goes to the lending company as compensation for that first year of no interest.

In this kind of purchase you and the store both win. The only loser is the credit company who will not benefit from your $250 interest. It is my humble opinion that if you can pay yourself for 28 months, you are further ahead than paying someone else for 36. In addition to the furniture being delivered to your home free and clear, you will have the discipline of putting $48 away each month and can continue this practice for the rest of your earning days.

Now that I have hopefully helped you see the reality that CREDIT EQUALS DEBT we can move on to the next immediate thought.

Can there really be such a thing as GOOD DEBT?

In a single word answer – YEP.

Somewhere in the paragraphs above I mentioned business debt, investment debt and mortgage debt. I also stated that if the borrower is serious about the reason for these kinds of debt there is nothing wrong with them.

To be serious about the reason for the debt I mean the borrower wants his business to succeed – he isn't simply borrowing money in the company name and spending it on his golf lessons or paying personal bills with it.

Rarely is investment debt as most people today think of it considered necessary. The bull market between 1982 and 2000 taught many people under the age of 40 that they needed to have their money in the stock market if they wanted it to see double-digit growth averages every year. Borrowing money to gamble on the stock market does not qualify as serious investment debt. The debt is serious, if your stocks drop you could lose everything they have pledged as collateral for the debt as many people did during a correction in the early 1980's and again in after the turn of the millennium.

Investment debt can qualify as good debt only if it also qualifies as business debt. If you borrow money to purchase a house to rent out with the serious anticipation the cash flow will result in an increase in your equity and net worth, than you have a good investment debt. But rental properties are a business and must be treated as such. They are not the quick return investment like the late 1970's when mortgage rates were low while real estate values climbing higher every month. That could happen again, but the possibility is very low.

Your house is shelter and as such it can make sense to purchase instead of renting a home. You must still justify the cost of owning your own home also so that it qualifies as good debt. Buy it too large and the maintenance and upkeep costs will eat you alive. Too small and your family will need to move early and the refinancing, the depressed housing market and a host of other snakes will bite you hard.

The total cost of your home, utilities, insurance, tax and mortgage should be less than 38% of your after tax income. An easier way to figure the maximum monthly payment you can make for a home is thus...

Take your after tax monthly income, multiply it by 28%(. 28). The resulting number is the most you can afford to pay on the mortgage of your home. If you are paying more than 28%, some other category in your budget is going to be making up the difference and it will catch up with you. It might work for a short time but before the mortgage is paid you will feel the pinch of financial pressures and the stress those pressures bring.

Save yourself the stress and avoid that kind of pressure, okay?

Consumer debt is always bad debt. So unless you can justify the debt as business, investment or mortgage the odds are strong the debt is not a good debt.

Of course there are always exceptions, so in those cases refer back to the four questions one must always ask themselves before signing on the dotted line to accept a new debt.

CHAPTER THREE–
FINANCIAL MANAGEMENT

Before we go further, what is Financial Management?

Simply put, it is managing finances. Ok, I used the words in the definition. So try this one on for size – Financial Management is the process a person has of controlling and making the most of their money.

One of the major reasons for financial management is the achievement of financial freedom. This is the point in time where you stop reading, look upwards and ask yourself 'Just what is financial freedom?'

Simply put, financial freedom is a state of mind relief that comes with the absence of worry and tension about overdue bills, a clear conscience before God and other people, and the knowledge you are ahead of the curve regarding finances and can survive just about any of the financial curveballs life may throw at you.

Financial management requires you to get your financial house in order. The most important part of setting your financial house in order is to get all of your outstanding bills currant (if any of your bills are behind) and then you must STAY current. This can include the electric bill, the car loan, a charge card bill, or any other type of debt you are currently carrying – up to and including your house payment. Everything must be paid up and current or else you will start out behind the eight ball and have a terribly difficult time getting to the goal of financial freedom.

PIECES OF THE FINANCIAL PUZZLE

To complete the picture of financial freedom it is required that eight pieces of the financial picture work together. These pieces are listed here:

1. A BUDGET – having a budget will enable you to determine how much money must be spent each month on NEEDS, how much is left for WANTS and DESIRES. We'll discuss these three parts of a budget later.

2. LIVING ESSENTIALS – look at what you believe are NEEDS each month and find ways to pare those costs to the minimum. Learn to substitute high cost goods with items none-brand-name items, or perhaps you can fix the leaky sink yourself instead of paying a plumber. Once the mindset is created to find inexpensive alternatives, it could become a fun challenge, a contest amongst family members to see who can find the least costly method or save the most money.

3. ALWAYS THINK BEFORE SPENDING – every purchase must be looked at through the window of (1) is it necessary, (2) does it reflect my ethics, (3) am I buying this item on impulse or is it really the best buy I can get, (4) does it depreciate quickly i.e. swimming pools, clothing, autos and etc. and also (5) what will it cost to maintain?

4. DO NOT BUY ANYTHING ON CREDIT – buying on a cash basis can cut as much as 33% from even a "bare-bones" budget! Also, bankruptcy and other drastic measures are only treating the symptom and not the problem. The problem is spending more than you take in. Get control of your financial life before the temptations of buying

on credit overwhelms you and your financial boat gets swamped a second time.

5.   AVOID LEVERAGE – this can be illustrated best by the example of a stock market portfolio. If you have $1000 in paper gains you can leverage that into control of $10000 worth of stocks. The upside sounds good, but if your investment fails, not only do you loose the investment you still owe the $9000 you leveraged. I realize that what I said earlier about investment as not qualifying as bad debt contradicts what I just said here about leverage. The qualifier here is the word leverage. If you are leveraging that debt, it is a bad debt. In fact you might as well be taking the money to the local casino and gambling with it. You have as good of chance of coming out ahead and you don't have the serious risk factor. If you take $1000 of your own money and borrow $9000 with the land as collateral then you have good investment debt. In the event you are unable to meet the payments, you return the land or the bank forecloses, and you loose only the money you have already paid. When you purchase real estate, always read the fine print and insist on a clause that allows you to give up the property to the lender without further compensation being required. This can be especially important in a depressed economic situation where the lender is unable to sell the property for enough money to cover your outstanding debt.

6.   SAVE! SAVE! SAVE! – Being disciplined in saving will carry you a long ways on the road to financial freedom. Even if you save a mere $10 a month, it is the training that is important. To paraphrase a portion of the Bible 'Who ever can be trusted with the small things can be trusted

with the larger things'. If you can save regularly a small amount of money then when you have a larger income you will be able to save proportionally larger amount.

7.   TITHE – this is the concept and idea of sharing at least 10% of your income with those people who are less fortunate. Even when you say 'I am the less fortunate' there is someone who needs help.

8.   GOD'S PROVISION – the final piece of the picture of financial freedom is to recognize and accept God is involved and will direct our lives if we let Him.

Financial management is very difficult without a Budget and financial freedom is for all practical intents and purposes IMPOSSIBLE. In the simplest manner, a budget IS financial planning. You will see where your money is going and decide how to make it go to satisfy your NEEDS, WANTS and DESIRES.

SPENDING OBJECTIVES

Anytime you spend a portion of your money you are satisfying one of 11 objectives. Ron Blue has put forth the idea, and my own observations agree that there are five short-term spending objectives and six long-term objectives.

In the short term your money can be …
1.   given away,
2.   spent on a lifestyle,
3.   repay a debt,
4.   pay taxes,
5.   saved.

In the long term you can spend your money on…
1.   financial independence,
2.   college education,
3.   debt repayment,
4.   charitable giving,
5.   major lifestyle desires,
6.   owning your own business.

It is number 5 on the long term spending objective list that makes each family and person unique. This major lifestyle desire could include a vacation home, some sort of special vacation, or any activity that is not currently being done.

Looking at the short-term goals, please note that 60% (3 out of 5) are consumptive in nature. Meaning of course that once you spend the money it is gone, out of here, adios. But the two remaining short-term objectives are actually productive. However what you Save grows in amount so that later you have more than when you started. Your money is producing money. Giving a portion of your money (tithing) is also productive in that you are helping others who are in need.

Of the long term spending objectives three are productive. Financial independence can be defined as meaning your accumulated resources funds the first four of your short-term objectives. Charitable giving is productive in the same manner for the long-term objectives as it was in the short term. If you don't remember why giving is productive, read the above paragraph.

The last long-term objective that is productive is owning your own business. Obviously if you own your own business you are an employer helping to support local families, you pay taxes, give charitably through your business and in general generate more money than the business costs on a monthly basis. This is called positive cash flow. If your business generates a negative cash flow for many months it is not productive but is in reality costing you precious resources. Be sure to watch the

budgetary portion of your business planning. If the business requires substantial inflows of new cash over a long period of time (generally considered to be twelve months) than you might want to revise your plan, cut
some costs, or find another business to be in.

If you have a business debt, or are planning on taking on business
debt make sure you have read the previous chapter about debt. Your
spouse must be part of the business operations even if all she does is listen
to your ideas. If you succeed your spouse will be there to encourage you,
and if your business dies your spouse will be there to encourage you and
help you try again. At all costs, though, DON'T hock the family home to
support a business. Your family will always need a place to live so it is not
advisable to mortgage the home to invest in a business.

Now back to the regularly intended line of writing. Financial
planning. Before you can do a proper budget you will need to determine
your spending objectives. Once this is accomplished integrate the 11
objectives into a four-step plan. Easier said than done, I know. But here is
the four-step plan laid out as easy as I can.

1.   What is your present situation?
2.   What are your financial goals?
3.   How can you increase your cash flow margin?
4.   How can you control your cash flow?

The first question (what is your present situation) can be answered
with a bit of pencil work (or computer if you do that sort of thing) and
paper. In this exercise you will be adding up your assets, subtracting liabilities and getting a snapshot of your net worth. A net worth is of course a
running total of all the financial transactions you have ever entered into.
So the goal is usually to have the net worth snap shot grow in relation to
your life goals and objectives.

FINANCIAL NET WORTH

Ready to begin? Here we go to get a financial snap shot of your net worth. Say cheese!

Start with liquid assets. These include anything you can quickly and easily turn into cash. The list can include – cash, short-term CD's, savings accounts, money market funds, life insurance cash values and anything more that has a ready market. A ready market for determining liquidity is measured by how much time will pass before you have exchanged your asset for cash.

If you can sell your asset and get cash in 48 hours or less, than it is a very liquid asset. If it takes you between a week and two weeks to convert your asset into cash, you have a semi-liquid asset. A non-liquid asset will take you two weeks or more to convert into cash.

Remember, you wan to get the actual value out of the asset. Anybody can sell their house for 50% of its value if they want the cash in a week. But unless you are running from somebody, that would me a very foolish thing to do.

An analogy would be to compare your assets to the different stages of water. For this analogy to work, consider water vapor to be cash and that is what you want to do, convert your assets to water vapor. Essentially all you have to do is to decide that you want cash instead of the asset and 'poof' you have cash. Of course some assets, like CD's, may not give you 100% of the value depending on the rules of the CD. If you have substantial penalties for early withdrawal, then what you have is a non-liquid asset. But if you can get 95% of the value out of the CD when you want to, than you have a liquid asset.

Semi-liquid assets are a bit harder to convert. They are like the actual water itself, before you can get water vapor you must heat the water and that takes time. It does take a bit of time to convert a semi-liquid asset to cash without suffering severe penalties. The object of course is to get all or almost all of your value out of the asset.

Then to finish our water analogy, non-liquid assets are the ice. More time is needed to convert these assets to cash because you have to melt the ice and then heat the water to get your water vapor.

To help you have a better idea of just what I am talking about (and in a desperate attempt to imitate the world famous finance authors) I have typed up a simple cash conversion chart for a couple we shall call Don & Dawn. They're your youngish American couple, Don works hard to provide a living and Dawn stays home with their two young children.

There's nothing fancy about it, all you have to do for your own Cash Conversion Chart (and to aid in figuring your own Net Worth) is simply write down every asset you own that someone else might be willing to give you cash for. Use the above listed guidelines to determine under which heading your asset will be listed. Beside the asset write down how much cash you seriously think you can get for the asset. I mean realistically, now. No big hopes.

The assets and their values I've listed are just a few pulled from thin air. These are not my assets in any way, shape or form!

On a side note here, I would title each of these charts more imaginatively but I really do not want anyone to get the idea that imagination is a good thing to have when working with their assets. You can imagine later for Financial Goals, but until then, please stick with reality.

Thanks.

Asset Value Chart

LIQUID ASSETS		
Cash	$100.00	
Savings Short-Term	$350.00	
Savings Long-Term	$550.00	
Subtotal		$1,000.00
SEMI-LIQUID ASSETS		
CD#1 – 3 month	$1,000.00	
CD#2 – 3 month	$1,000.00	
Subtotal		$2,000.00
NON-LIQUID ASSETS		
Stamp Collection	$1,250.00	
House	$65,000.00	
Auto	$3,000.00	
Subtotal		$69,250.00
ASSET VALUE		$72,250.00

That's easy, right? It looks like Don and Dawn are doing okay.

Now that you have your liquid asset total you need to add the nonliquid asset total as I show in the above illustration. As we just discussed non-liquid assets are those assets not easily turned into cash, or require more than a 5% loss in value to get the cash. Your home, land, business valuation, boat, camper, auto, furniture, antiques, coin collections, IRA's, pension and debts others owe to you. You may have more or you may have less than this list, but add up everything you could turn into cash no matter how long you think it might take you to do the actual conversion.

The total of liquid and non-liquid assets is your Asset Value.

Now calculate your liabilities. A liability is anything that is not an asset (what else would it be?) and this is also called debt.

Credit cards, furniture & auto & personal loans, mortgage, and any other amount of money you owe to somebody or some company. This total is called your Liability. You can create a Liability chart like this one for Don & Dawn.

Chart of Liabilities

LIABILITIES	
Auto Loan	$1,000.00
Mortgage	$39,000.00
Borrowed from Dad	$5,000.00
Total Liability	$45,000.00

Liabilities never look very good, of course. But just how bad are things really? Let's keep on working those calculators.

Subtract your liability total from your Asset Value. See the number there? Hopefully it is a positive one. If not, you are in trouble and need to really work out a plan to get those debts paid off. You have a longer road towards financial freedom than most.

That number you have left over after subtracting your Liabilities from your Asset Value is called your Net Worth. That is what your possessions are actually worth as cash.

Here's another chart for that illustration. If you haven't guessed, I have just recently figured out how to do this sort of thing easily and still get the book printer to not charge extra to have these charts in my manuscript.

Net Worth Chart

NET WORTH CALCULATION	
ASSET VALUE	$72,250.00
LIABILITY	$45,000.00
NET WORTH	$27,250.00

All of a sudden that $72,250 does not look so good, does it? One of the things this exercise can tell us is that 62 cents of every dollar Don & Dawn have in assets has been bought with debt. I'm not going to throw stones at them and say this is a bad thing, but it is certainly not good. If this is all they truly have in liability, than they can survive. But if they start a regimen of credit card spending, or acquiring more debt, they will soon find their little Net Worth of $27,250.00 gone.

You can also call this Net Worth paper by a different name – a Balance Sheet. This is an authorized name because you have written out (legibly) your Assets and your Liabilities. The difference between the two is a balance. The Asset side has got to be weighted heavier than the Liability side if you are to have much hope of achieving financial freedom.

I heard a recent statistic to the effect that the typical multimillionaire had a net worth of only $150,000 excluding their home. For someone with said to have that much money and then find out that they are actually worth 'only' $150,000 is scary. But if you live a luxurious lifestyle there is often not much money left over for accumulation and growth.

Having someone call you frugal is not an insult but a compliment. Frugality is what keeps the net worth growing. Net worth must grow until you achieve your financial goals. Accumulation without a stopping point is not smart.

FINANCIAL GOALS

Now on to the second question—what are your financial goals? A financial goal can be anything relating to money, no matter how improbable it may seem. Goals are not strict controls to live your life by, but more like guidelines.

A financial goal can include just about anything. Take a vacation to Europe, go on a four month missionary trip to the people of Mexico, or perhaps you want to bequest a million dollars to your local correctional institution. Sit down and make a list today and as you think of more in the coming days and months ahead, add those goals to your list. The key is keeping your goal sheet in mind when you are spending time fine-tuning your financial plans. Have I mentioned that yet? A financial plan is something you need to work on a few hours a month to fine tune, keep in balance and steer towards accomplishing your goals.

Now for the reasons it is important to make and set goals for yourself and family.

1. GOALS GIVE DIRECTION AND PURPOSE – with goals you have something tangible to work towards while also having a place to finish. It is not very difficult to tell when you have accomplished your goal.
2. GOALS CRYSTALLIZE THINKING – when you write down your goal your thinking becomes clearer, both in

what exactly your goal is and in how to work to reach that goal.

3.   GOALS MOTIVATE – with a goal you have something to work for, a reason to work. Without motivation many people tend to float along like a jellyfish in the ocean; whichever way the currents are going that day is where they go spending money along the way.

4.   GOALS STATE THE FUTURE – since only God knows the future then our making out a list of goals to accomplish are implicitly a statement saying "God willing, I believe I will accomplish…"

So why doesn't everybody set goals instead of those who seem successful in life?

1.   WE FEAR FAILURE – if we actually set a few goals in our life and then are unable to attain those goals, it is human to feel that we failed.

2.   WE ASSUME GOAL SETTING TAKES TIME – and it does. Everyday we dream about a goal we'd like to accomplish. Goal setting is the actual process of taking a few minutes of the day on occasion and putting those thought goals onto paper.

3.   WE DON'T KNOW WHAT GOALS TO SET – there are so many 'experts' running around telling us what we should do with our money, our time, our families that it is easy to be confused. That is where the writing of the goals comes in – if you write it you can take the time to write the goal down, you can crystallize how to achieve that goal and if it is a goal worth having.

You can go on to the next question if you want, but it will not be a bad thing to sit quietly right here for a minute and dream about what you would like to do. Got that picture in your head? Write it down. That's your first financial goal. Does that mean you must complete that goal first? No. But the first step is to write down all your financial goals from silly to superb. Combine them with the goals from the rest of your family and then determine the order in which to accomplish these goals.

Okay, you've sat and thought long enough. You'll have more time to do this goal setting a little later. For now, read on.

INCREASE YOUR CASH FLOW

Now for question number three – How can you increase your cash flow margin? Positive cash flow is vitally important for financial planning. You can plan with a negative cash flow but there your goals are to cut spending, increase your cash margin and repay your debts so you can get out of the red before it is too late. Now we are past that point and back into the black, even if your net worth is zero it is never too late to start growing your net worth total. And a positive cash flow margin is totally necessary. Even neutral cash flow is not good enough. All a neutral cash flow says is your income is just meeting your outgo. If your child gets sick and you miss an hour of work to take her to the doctor you not only have a $50 doctor bill (at minimum) you also are going to be short $5 (at minimum) in your next paycheck. Then suddenly your cash flow is negative again. Not a good thing to have happen.

Thus as you can now so clearly observe a positive cash flow is vital for financial planning and your financial success. At the least a positive cash flow is building a safety cushion for such a scenario as I just laid out in the paragraph above.

Meanwhile, back on how to increase a cash flow margin.

The easiest and best return for your money method of increasing cash flow is to decrease spending. Start with decreasing your living expenses. Go back to the pieces of the big picture of financial freedom. Look at LIVING ESSENTIALS and ALWAYS THINK BEFORE SPENDING. The little bits of advice and ideas you glean from those paragraphs can help you start reducing living expenses.

Why not get a second job, get a raise, or do something else to bring in more income? Why not indeed! First of all, there is nothing wrong with working harder or earning more income. But if you are a mother of young children I firmly believe those kids come first and need their mother (or father) at home when they are home. It is the best way to raise the next generation to be good stewards of what they have, the best ways to play and get along as well as an entire world full of knowledge kids need before leaving the house. It is important to remember after all that we are not raising children, we are teaching the next generation of adults.

So that lecture over, if both parents working is the only possible way to get out of debt than you do what you have to do. But make a promise to each other, right it on the refrigerator door, that all income from the second spouse goes into the debt repayment and once the debt is done, the spouse returns to being a stay at home parent – at least until all the children are in school and then if desired the spouse is free to get a part time job when the kids are at school.

Okay, that's the last time I yap about one spouse staying home with the children. I'd promise but I can't guarantee a thing, understand?

Let's put yourself into the shoes of Don and say he is earning $24,000 and for this example paying 15% taxes (I'm including Social Security, and any other tax your area puts on you, I'm figuring your income tax will be negligible because of deductions). Mister Don (like you) wants to have another $2000 in Discretionary spending. To achieve this he must earn at least $2300. If you tithe you will need to earn $2650 extra just to take home and spend an additional $2027. Now I don't know about you but when the average wage increase is less than 5% the chances of Don's income taking an at least 11% jump is probably easily calculated at less than zero. You have as good of chance as Don.

Figure Increased Discretionary Money

ANNUAL INCOME		$24,000.00
Desired Increase		$ 2640.00
Less Tax 15%		$ 394.00
Less Tithe 10%	$	225.00
New Spending Money	$	2027.00

Again, it is far easier to decrease spending than it is to increase income. Plus every dollar you don't spend is one entire dollar going to increase your cash flow. For every dollar you earn in additional income you only get to take home 76 cents of it.

That tidbit is just a little something to keep in mind during your next round of financial planning.

EVERYTHING ELSE (SO FAR)

The final question deals with controlling your cash flow and that is answered through the actual financial plan and the ultimate end result – A BUDGET! Yes, we are going to talk about that dreaded B-word. But that comes later, not just yet.

Let me think a minute here and see what else would fall under the category of FINANCIAL MANAGEMENT. So far I think we have done wonderful in covering a few of the basic thoughts and ideas.

—-INTERMISSION—-

I'm back so let's continue on.

COMMUNICATION

One of the most important aspects to remember about financial management (especially if you are married) is to communicate with your spouse. You have to keep in mind that if your spouse does not support your financial plans than all the planning the world won't help.

Survey after survey has found that women are more inclined to exercise restraint and have a fear of being in debt – this is contrary to the normal stereotype. Also the woman seeks help when she sees she is in trouble faster than a man will. A man's indifference, pride or optimism keeps him from seeking help as soon as a problem appears. Also many serious debts can directly be linked to and are the result of the husbands spending or poor financial decision making.

If the wife and husband team are not communicating, these natural and normal difference between them will actually split their marriage apart and could land them in divorce court. Of course there are other reasons as well, but money problems are sited as the number one reason for their arguments and ultimately divorce in over 70% of all divorce! Don't be a statistic—communicate. Yelling is communicating if you stop and listen to what your spouse is yelling. Communication is easier once the yelling is over and the husband and wife have gotten over the emotional aspect and are willing to actually talk and listen to each other.

USE TEAMWORK TO MANAGE YOUR MONEY

The first thing you need to recognize is that different is not bad or inferior. A husband and wife union is frequently described as a team because it is a team. Many times when the two are working together the wife is the counselor – and the husband is the doer. Not always is this the case, but frequently it is.

Whichever spouse is the best suited to keeping the checkbook and the books should. But when it comes to paying bills – do them together! The one who handles the checkbook writes the checks, the other says who is being paid, how much and then seals the envelopes. Teamwork.

Financial goals for the family must be set together and they must be specific. Often you will need to compromise with your spouse when it comes to goal setting. Nobody in the family will always get everything that they want. When you reach an impasse STAY CALM! Emotions are wonderful things but they are not good financial decision makers. Work to find a solution to the impasse you both can live with. One possibility is to have both spouses list five positions about their side of the issue from worst to best. Both discard the first and the last and then you will at least have a framework to work within to reach a compromise.

The experts who ask the right kind of questions have reported that generally speaking 'financial worries and problems are caused by a lack of management skills'. All that we have talked about in this chapter deals with financial management. As a nation we have one of the highest literary levels in the world. But when it comes to financial literacy we don't do so well. Our children spend 16 years in school learning how to earn an income while excluding family training, they will generally receive less than 6 weeks instruction in how to control and grow that income.

There is no shame in being illiterate if you are willing to admit your lack of ability and resolve to actually do something about correcting this problem. Seek help from a financial professional. But beware, there are many scam artists out there who are willing to help themselves by claiming to be able to help you. The trouble is that they aren't helping you with anything except to throw away a lot of dough. Get references, ask tons of questions, and don't buy financial products from an advisor who is also selling those products if he receives any financial incentive for pushing those products.

Ask the advisor about how he is paid, most states have legal requirements of disclosure about how financial advisors are paid. The ones to avoid are those who are commission compensated. Salaried advisors usually don't have a large interest in selling you a product just because they can; they are usually motivated by a desire to actually help you and your finances.

It is extremely important to recognize the need to be financially smart and then develop the skills you will need to use your financial resources wisely. Read books, talk to other people who have been there, seek counsel. Just keep your eyes open and try to avoid being bilked. Occasionally a bilker will succeed in making you a bilkee, but it should not happen more than once.

Like I said a few paragraphs ago, you need to work with your spouse in developing financial plans. Lets go through this process of organizing and preparing yourselves for the financial planning and budgeting process.

First thing to do is sit down on a quiet evening with your spouse and a stack of paper, pens, pencils, calculators, and nourishment. Do not try to do this with your children awake. Do not do this after a stressful day at the end of which you came home and kicked the cat.

KEEP EXCELLENT RECORDS
(you never know when the IRS will knock)

We've already talked about determining where you are financially. Get that Balance Sheet (Net Worth) paper out again. You've lost it already? Well, make another one.

You should set up a filing system of some sort to keep your records and expense receipts in. It could be a shoebox to a four-drawer state of the art, automatic lock, fingerprint ID required, fireproof, theft resistant, security alarm rigged filing cabinet. It doesn't matter as long as you know where the information can be found at any given time.

Into your filing system will go a copy of your completed tax return and all the information you may need to justify your deductions in case you are audited. You will also want to include your checkbook register (it is a good idea to start a new register every year), W-2 forms, tax receipts, investment receipts, etc.

Don't forget to include any home improvement receipts as you improve your home these will help to lower taxable gains on the sale of your home someday. It is a good idea to store bank account numbers, insurance policy information, business records, medical information, etc in this filing system as well. If there is ever an emergency or something happens to you this information will be easily found. Make sure you update the information annually.

Now that the information is organized and you have your Balance Sheet written out so as to be able to read it and thus can see where you are financially, let's go on. First thing is to look at the balance sheet and see what kind of shape your finances are in. If the liabilities are overwhelming the assets, look at the liabilities and see what kind they are. Good debt will provide assets that grow in value and of course a new mortgage will skew the balance sheet towards the negative. Consumer debt is bad debt because the purchased items are used up and don't grow in value – in other words you are paying for a hole in the ground. Stop creating that kind of debt and make sure the number one priority of your financial plan is repayment of bad debt. If you fail to pay off your debt, it will skew your balance sheet out of proportion and ultimately will crash any financial plan that does not repay this kind of debt as soon as possible.

Okay, you have the quiet time, the supplies and your spouse. It is time to get down to the task and develop some financial goals. After those lovely little items we will talk about the heart of this entire book – a BUD-GET.

CHAPTER FOUR– FINANCIAL PLANS

How does a person go about developing financial plans? We've talked about a few of the necessary items you will need to use. That is your paper, pencils, calculator, and your mind. We are constantly thinking about financial goals; the problem is often times these goals don't get written down and thus never incorporated into our financial plans.

Perhaps now is a good time to actually explain just what a financial plan is. I know I'm this far into the book and have talked about financial goals and plans before. But now this is what those terms mean.

FINANCIAL GOAL – a dream regarding where you want to spend your money

FINANCIAL PLAN – the method by which you will fulfill your goal

There, that sounds simple enough doesn't it? According to Mr. Webster a goal is 'an objective, the purpose toward which effort is directed'. That sounds about right, doesn't it? If you want to go on that cruise to the South Pacific you will have to direct your efforts to making that happen.

On the other hand, a plan is nothing more than 'a method to accomplish an objective'. Well what do you know? A GOAL and a PLAN go hand in hand. If all you have is a goal, than your dream will remain just that – a dream.

Back to that first question of this chapter – how does a person go about making financial plans? First you have got to write down your financial goals. What are they? Take some time, an hour, a day, maybe a week or even a month. But kick back and let your mind wonder where it will. Make sure everyone in the family does this as well. The breadwinner cannot be the only one to do all the work.

Do you have your financial goals? Write them down, along with those from everyone else. Take a look at them and see what they are. Vacations, different house, your own business or maybe just a bit of savings.

Remember to make your GOALS measurable. If it is a trip to Tahiti, than you will measure your progress by how much money you have saved for the journey. If you do not have a measurable goal, say 'I want to retire comfortably', then how will you know when you have achieved your goal? Or how will you know when you are half way done, or perhaps you might discover a need to set aside more if you have a measurable goal.

Think about it and it will make sense.

The hardest part about the setting of financial goals is arranging them into a semblance of priority. It would be nice if all the goals could be worked towards at the same time but in this reality we call life you have to have priorities.

Be sure you have written all your goals down before doing more with them than reading the next section. Goals will change over time, that's fine. But just as your Net Worth is a snapshot of your finances, so are the Goals a snapshot of your dreams at this given place in time.

PRIORITY GOAL – REMOVE ALL DEBT

So look at the list compiled from your own dreams and those of your family. If you still have any consumer debts to pay and that also includes an auto loan or money borrowed from a relative, than you have just figured out your first priorities. Get rid of unproductive debt – again this is the bad debt we've talked about earlier.

Place a numeral one (1) beside the smallest consumer debt. The next smallest consumer debt gets the numeral two (2) and so on and so forth down the list until you no longer have any consumer debts unmarked. Why, you are likely asking, do you start with the smallest debt first? Shouldn't you be paying off the highest interest rate?

Many people and advisors will tell you to stop paying those high interest rates by paying off those debts first. But I say if you do that then you are spreading yourself around instead of concentrating your resources on individual targets. If you can, move those high interest rates to lower interest rates either with the same company or through another lending institution. There, that takes care of your high interest rate concerns.

Please note – the following illustrative example will work best on a short-low minimum debt. If you have a short-high minimum debt, plug those numbers into the formula to see which debt should be paid off first.

Now pay off that smallest debt first. Let's say you owe $50 a month on one debt and it will be paid off in 24 months and $75 on a debt to be paid off in 30 months. When month number 25 rolls around you only have one debt left to pay. Take the $50 that had been going to the first debt and apply it along with the $75 to the second debt. Now instead of having to pay $75 for five more months you are going to pay $125 for three months. You have just saved yourself THREE MONTHS of pay-ments! Of course these numbers are made up and if you do still have con-sumer debts, the actual savings of time could be much, much larger. If you have an additional $25 a month to put towards the first debt you would

save eight (8) months of payments on the first debt and you will be finished with both repayment plans a whopping SEVEN MONTHS early.

If you work it this way you started with a debt load totaling $3450
to be paid in thirty months. By adding only $25 a month above the mini-
mums and paying off the smallest debt first and then adding those payments to help pay off the second debt, you will end those thirty months
with $1050 in savings.

Imagine what you can do with $1050.

Here's the original payment schedule you would have of paying
just the minimum payment each and every month as required.

Payment Chart #1

	Balance	Payment	Time	Total Months
Debt #1	$1,200.00	$50.00	24	24
Debt #2	$2,250.00	$75.00	30	30

And here's how the payment schedule would look if you paid off
the smallest debt first (Debt #1) and then applied that amount towards
the Debt #2. Notice how you will cut the time to repay by 10%. Not a
bad incentive, wouldn't you agree?

Payment Chart #2

	Balance	Payment	Time	Total Months
Debt #1	$1,200.00	$50.00	24	24
Debt #2	$2,250.00	$75.00	30	27

Finally for this section of examples, here is a simple illustration of what would be the result if you took an additional $25 and applied it first towards Debt #1 and then all of that payment went to pay off Debt #2 early.

Payment Chart #3

	Balance	Payment	Time	Total Months
Debt #1	$1,200.00	$75.00	24	16
Debt #2	$2,250.00	$75.00	30	23

It's one thing to read about how paying off your small debt first and then applying the monthly payment amount towards the next largest debt will save you time and ultimately money. But to see it displayed out in a simple chart is even better. Just imagine what would happen if you used this method to fund your Financial Goals. Wow!

Payment Chart #4 (this one's paying yourself)

Loan	Payment	Months	Amount Saved
$0.00	$150.00	7	$1,050.00

That last chart was a bit more difficult to draw up so anyone could just glance at it and understand. But I think I did it. If not, and you are confused as to what that chart is all about, reread the preceding pages. If you don't want to do that, then this chart represents what will happen if you add $25.00 a month to Debt #1, and when that is done to add that payment to Debt #2. When this is paid off, take the $150.00 monthly payment and stuff it into savings (assuming you have not other debts). This will leave you with a net gain of $1050.00 at the end of your original debt payoff period of 30 months.

Neat, huh?

But it took two and a half years you say. That is something you will encounter every time you set goals. They take TIME! Just about everybody has 50 good years to set goals and accomplish them. That is a fair amount of time so working a year or two towards accomplishing an objective is not unreasonable.

Put it another way, if you put $150 each and every month into a savings account (or your mattress though I don't endorse that idea) for that entire 50 years you would net a principle amount (being without interest) totaling $90000. I realize this number has no value or use to our discussion but I thought you might like that little tidbit for the next party you attend and the small talk stalls out.

Take another look at that list of financial goals. All the consumer debts should have a number listing them in order of smallest to greatest. What about the remainder of your list? Do you have less than 10 goals written down—if so go back to dreamland and dream up a few more goals to write down. If you have over one hundred good for you even though there is a strong chance you will not get them all accomplished.

Everyone in the family should be in agreement about which goals are take priority on the list. Of course agreement can be difficult and compromise may be necessary but it can be done. Be sure to take a few minutes for a break whenever someone starts throwing things. This phase of the financial management should be reasonably fun – these are your dreams and goals after all.

Keep in mind that this list of financial goals will be going into your filing system and you will want to update at least once every year. I would recommend that you do not update your goals more than twice a year though. If you change the goals to many times, you will never get any of them accomplished.

As time passes you will find that today's goals are not as important next year or next decade. Be sure to date the list whenever you change it, over time it may prove interesting to see how the families priorities changed.

THE COST OF HAVING GOALS

Do you have all your goals prioritized? Good, now how much is each one going to cost? In addition is there a time limit you have to work within? Keep the time restraints in mind when you estimate the costs of accomplishing each goal. Write down the estimated cost beside the goal. You can always adjust the estimated cost later if inflation or the cost of college or some such thing goes up (down would be surprising, wouldn't it).

This is where the work gets tricky. If you do have consumer debt you will know how much each month the minimum to pay is. These numbers (assuming you have more than one debt) will be placed directly into your budget. As for the rest of your financial goals, you will need to work your budget first to determine how much surplus you have available. If your budget is so tight you have nothing left over as surplus, then you need to either forego achieving your financial goals or cut costs to provide enough surplus cash to start working towards your goals.

SPENDING DECISIONS

I use the word surplus and discretionary income to mean the same thing. To be honest your necessities are not all that different today than they were a century ago. Every body needs (thus I call these the 3 NECESSITIES)...

1. Food,
2. Home,
3. Utilities (no you don't need running water or sewer if you live in the countryside, but good sanitation cuts down on doctor or mortician bills and thus saves money in the long run)

Every dollar that does not buy one of these three things is discretionary spending. You might think you have to have money to buy gas for your car to get to work, but it is at your description that you live where you live and work where you work. Nobody has told you to live here and work way over there.

A telephone, television, Internet, and even clothing are all discretionary spending. A very radical concept I must admit and if you are going to forego the expenditure of money on clothing I would suggest you do not live in Nebraska – you'll get frostbite on your sunburn. But despite what society and culture tells us about our purchases, everything we spend our money on beyond the three listed is at our discretion—keep that in mind when you go shopping the next time for some object you "just have to have".

If you were to get even more nitpicky and look at what you spend in each of the three categories you could probably save money there as well. Remember – every dollar you can cut from your current spending is one more dollar going straight into your cash flow.

So lets look at FOOD. If you live alone you most likely eat out a lot. Buying food from restaurants or prepackaged costs more than if you take the ingredients home and cook them yourself. Even if you (and I mean families as well) do already cook most of your meals at home, start buying the meat that the law requires the store to throw away that day. This is usually tossed early in the morning. Don't forget to ask about those dented can specials. Or the mystery label sale. Do not descend to the level of dumpster diving unless you are ready to wear the label of miser. These other money saving suggestions can earn you the right to call yourself frugal, but a miser is not a positive label to wear.

What about HOME? Sell that 1800 square foot (more or less) palace and contact the real estate agent. Tell them you want the least expensive house they can find in or out of the city limits. More than likely this will be next to a smelly industry or across from the state penitentiary but don't worry. I'm told you get used to the odor or the lights soon enough. Look at what you could save on entertaining guests!

UTILITIES can also be cut to the bare basics. Live in a warm climate without air conditioning and go to bed when the sun goes down and you can't see outside because the it is the new moon phase and totally dark. Of course, one of the things to watch for here is that in the olden days before electricity many families had ten children for a reason. At the very least, don't forget to turn off the lights when you leave a room and crank the heat down when you are gone for more than a day. Like a said, good sanitation helps prevent disease so running water and sewer are important necessities.

Some people would insist that taxes should be one of those necessary spending requirements. I disagree because if there were no government agency to collect the tax, would you still have to pay it? In order to live you must have home, heat, and food. So I have taken the liberty of sticking the tax question under the heading of discretionary spending.

REMEMBER THE SPENDING OBJEC-
TIVES

Now that I have you completely shook up and looking at your spending habits in a different light (sunlight of course), it's time for a little review. Remember back in the last chapter I told you that any time you spend any of your money for any reason you are satisfying one of 11 objectives.

To refresh your memory the 5 short-term objectives for money are to be...

1.   given away,
2.   spent on a lifestyle,
3.   repay a debt,
4.   pay taxes,
5.   saved.

In the long term you can spend your money on...

1.   financial independence,
2.   college education,
3.   debt repayment,
4.   charitable giving,
5.   major lifestyle desires,
6.   owning your own business.

I will also take the time here to point out that 60% (3 out of 5) of the short-term objectives are still consumptive in nature. Meaning of course that once you spend the money it is gone, out of here, adieus. Only the category of SPENT ON A LIFESTYLE is spending required for living. That means the other four are discretionary. Once you satisfy the lifestyle everything else is surplus.

Of course, using your discretionary spending in a productive manner is always good. Pay attention to the two productive objectives when you are planning your budget. It is these that will do you more good emotionally and spiritually than any of the others. The first is saving your surplus. What you save grows in amount over time so that later you have more than when you started. Your money is producing money. Being a good steward of your resources requires you to both make the effort to wisely use what God has given us and to share our resources with others. You can also consider yourself as spending productively when you give a portion of your money (tithing) away because it is sowing resources to help others in need.

An optimist would say that what you are sharing might be the amount needed to help someone back on their feet so that they can become productive members of society and start paying taxes and sharing their resources with others as well. Kind of like a pyramid scheme, one person helps two who help four who help eight. You get the picture, that's the optimistic outlook. A lot of people give for religious reasons and because it makes them feel good to be part of the solution and not the problem.

Obviously the long term spending objective of owning your own business is extremely productive because then you are an employer helping to support local families, paying taxes, give charitably through your business and in general generating more money income than the business outflow requires on a monthly basis. This is called positive cash flow. If your business generates a negative cash flow for many months it is of course not productive and is a consumptive objective. You are throwing precious resources down a hole. Be sure to watch this hole and if the future does not look good for eventual positive cash flow and/or will require substantial inflows of new cash over the long term than you might want to revise your business plan, cut some costs, or get out of the business all together.

Major lifestyle desires can be anything from your financial goal list that requires a long-term effort (long term financially is usually over 1 year in length). This includes a second home, early retirement or a special vacation.

The one dream just about every person shares with every one else – even if they won't admit it – is financial independence and this term is frequently interchanged with financial freedom. They are not the same thing and should not be used the same. Just about everyone dreams of financial freedom – the absence of worry about finances that comes with being ahead of the curve when it comes to life's curveballs and of course, the worry about how to pay bills. Financial Independence takes this thought even further and unties your money from anyone else's shirttails. You are making your own money in sufficient quantity that you can work if you want to, not work if you don't want to, and fund all of your spending objectives at any level of spending you want.

Basically if you are financially independent you are rich. For some – of course – rich might be $250,000 if they live simply and modestly. For other who have expensive tastes and think they need only the most costly goods, rich might not even be $25,000,000. Rich is a state of mind.

Financial freedom has become a catchall phrase for every huckster and shyster selling you a get rich quick scheme. Avoid these guys for the only ones getting rich quick are them and that's by taking your money. True financial independence occurs when you have accumulated enough resources to fund your short-term objectives and at such a time you are financially independent you will also note that you can fund your long term spending objectives as well.

This is as good of item as any to give you an example of a few Financial Goals – written for Don and Dawn, of course.

Financial Goal Chart

1.	Vacation in Disneyland in 3 years—$3,000.00
2.	New Computer in six months—$800.00
3.	Repaint Kitchen—$125.00
4.	Relocate to Hawaii in ten years—$8,000.00

As you can now see, Financial Goals do not have to be cheap, easy, or boring. Dream, dream big, dream small, and strive to achieve your dreams.

Let's review what you will need for the next chapter, which is coming up real soon here. First things first you need your pencil and pen and paper. I suggest both pen and pencil so when you break the lead on the pencil you don't have to go looking for a sharpener. Make sure your paper supply is still quit thick. Anytime I start attempting to figure numbers on paper it takes at least a dozen sheets. Maybe more if this is your first serious attempt at the Financial Management Process.

By this time you should also have your Balance Sheet written out (yes, I am still harping on that even though we did not use it in this chapter) – do make sure your handwriting is readable and the numbers actually balance. Check the calculations one more time, just to be sure. You'll be advised to use the calculator you were supposed to have found earlier. If you are using an adding machine, fine. I use a simple calculator from the local dollar store.

You've got supplies and your Balance Sheet and don't forget the sheet(s) upon which you have written out in proper order of priority your Financial Goals. If you do have current consumer debt (if you do this should be the top priority) make sure you have the minimum amounts due each month so you can plug these numbers directly into your budget.

If you have all these I think you are probably ready to actually develop your budget. Remember a budget is nothing more than a guideline of how you are going to spend you money and will not take care of your pennies, but will enable you to more wisely spend the dollar bills that enter your life each month.

Got all your stuff together yet? If you are ready, let's go on to the next chapter.

One moment of interruption here before I continue. For those of you who did as I suggested in this chapter – wrote out your financial goals with yourself, your spouse and your family and then prioritized them in order to accomplish – congratulations. That page or pages of prioritized goals (get rid of consumer debt is number one) is more than just a list. It is a complete financial plan.

Yep. That's right. You have written a financial plan you can follow. I know you can follow it because you did the thinking, the prioritizing and the cost estimation. Now take it onto the Budget.

CHAPTER FIVE–
THE BUDGET

The moment you have been waiting for is finally here. We are now going to discuss and attempt to detail how you can go about drawing a map customized for your own financial road. I have already told you what to bring to the budgeting table so you are prepared and I doubt you will need to be told again. But just in case someone has picked up this book and skipped all the preparation work in the previous chapters, I'll list what you need again.

Yourself, your spouse if you are married, pens, paper, pencils, calculator, balance sheet, financial goals and your financial plan. If you are like the majority of people today the idea that you have an actual workable financial plan is in itself a very big accomplishment. You have done something many people only dream about.

Now, armed with your roadmap in hand it is time to take that first step towards financial freedom. You are ready to begin hammering out a budget that will accomplish your financial goals and keep you in the black – at the same time.

HOW MUCH YOU REALLY BRING
HOME

Step one is to start with a blank sheet of paper. It could have lines if you wish, but lines are not necessary unless you think nice and neat appearances are worth something. Somewhere towards the top left hand corner write GROSS INCOME. Below this write in the total compensation the breadwinner will receive in a twelve-month period. A breadwinner is properly described by Mr. Webster as "one whose income is the primary support for dependants". Whether husband or wife, the spouse who grosses the most income in a year (determine this by looking at the W-2 forms every employer is required to give out once a year prior to January 31) is the breadwinner.

Now write down the second income below the first income. Remember these incomes right now are to be GROSS INCOME only. A gross income is called that not because it is so ugly small but because it is what you earn before taxes, deductions, automatic payments, etc. are removed.

Do you have any other income besides W-2 income? If so, the gross income from this other income needs to be written in this column as well. We need an honest budget and the only way to do that is to document all income and all expenses. Tedious, yes but don't worry it will all be worthwhile in the end.

Total your GROSS INCOME column and write this figure at the bottom of the column. Get out your calculator and divide your ANNUAL GROSS INCOME amount by twelve (12). Twelve is of course the number of months in a year. Take the number you got from dividing GROSS INCOME by twelve. Circle it or underline it or something so you know it is the total and when you look at it later. This is your MONTHLY GROSS INCOME.

I must make mention here that I am writing this to guide you in developing a budget for a monthly basis. It is my experience that paying bills once a month and dividing up the loot once a month is easier than trying to remember that 'this bill is paid this week, but next week we need to take out more than that for such and such a thing'. I am not saying you cannot build a budget that will work on a weekly or bi-weekly basis. Doing it that way simply requires more work and effort on your part.

Anybody who knows me recognizes the fact that I prefer to do as little work as necessary to get the task accomplished properly.

Take a look at your MONTHLY GROSS INCOME. You will now proceed to demolish it bit by bit, dollar by dollar, until all you have left is your net monthly income.

This part can be tricky unless you know the percentages of the taxes removed. You can also use the amounts removed each of the last four months but do be sure that your income has remained the same each month. If it has there is a way to divide what was withheld (legal stealing by the government) by your gross paycheck. For Social Security you should see a number resembling 6.2%. Your employer pays half of the government mandated total and the number you see as having been deducted from your paycheck is the half you are required to pay. The Medicare portion of your employment tax totals 1.25%, again that is merely half of what the government requires. Your employer has to pay the rest.

I guess you could look at this as a 7.65% wage you don't ever see, even though supposedly you will see it when you turn 65 or 67, or maybe 70. That number depends on what number Congress decides is acceptable for you to stop working at.

Just a note, when you look at your paycheck stub that shows the deductions, your Social Security and Medicare might be under a heading called FICA.

Now you know how much must be withheld from each paycheck you receive. Sad, isn't it. There is little or nothing you can do to lower these payroll taxes short of earning less income.

Please note—if you are self-employed your taxes are calculated a bit different in the sense that you pay all of your Social Security tax as well as the Medicare taxes. Don't worry though, this budget making process is designed for the typical person who receives the same amount of income every month and most likely you have set up a system whereby you pay yourself a base amount each and every month. If you don't do this already, you should because it will make your financial life simpler. If you do already pay yourself a base amount each month than read on with sanity – the suggestions here will work for you as well as they work for the W-2 earner.

In a column titled WITHHOLDINGS list the three payroll taxes and how much is withheld each and every month. You will also need to insert INCOME TAX and how much is withheld every month. I realize that many, many people receive hundreds of dollars as income tax refunds every year and treat this money as though it is 'found money'.

Fools.

TAX REFUND – THE GREAT SCAM

Unless their refund is really coming from the Earned Income Credit they have been over paying their taxes. No bid deal, right? After all if you pay too much then you don't have to worry about the IRS under-payment penalties and audits and things like that.

Wrong. You may still get audited and things like that are bound to happen no matter if your taxes are over paid or not. Let's see what the costs of over paying the IRS a measly $100 a month are going to be.

You pay $100 every month. If you had that money to put in the bank at 5% interest (I'd use 12% like many financial authors do to make your returns look more impressive except I doubt most people can get more than 5% on their money guaranteed) you would earn $32 interest. You can calculate this by taking $100 and multiplying it by 5% for $5 interest a year. Divide that by 12 months and there you have the interest on $100 at 5% for one month – an entire whopping 42 cents. Since we're talking about a year here how many months worth of interest would you earn? Answer. 78. You get this by adding 12 plus 11 plus 10 plus 9 ... plus 3 plus 2 plus 1.

This declining addition is of course the amount of time each $100 can earn interest. Take the 78 and multiply it by 42 cents. As you have probably heard many times by now, if you over pay your taxes are making an interest free loan to the government. Which is completely true. Worse, it is costing you money. You are losing the $32 annual interest and you are losing the control of $1200. Of course you will get it back next April but gee, why not have your money now instead of later? Not very many people would refuse to take an extra $100 in their monthly paycheck. That's like $3 a day, weekends included, for doing nothing more than changing your W-4's to reflect your true income tax withholding allowances. Check it out. I'm not here to tell you how to completely revamp your taxes or anything but do try to get your tax bill as small as possible. Your budget will thank you.

BASIC NECESSITY SPENDING

Now where were we? Oh yeah – at your WITHHOLDING column. Total up your withholdings. Social Security, Medicare and Income taxes are all withholdings. Write this number down and circle it.

Take up your calculator again and punch in your MONTHLY GROSS INCOME number. Subtract the number you just wrote into the WITHHOLDING column. Take a good look at the new number. Write that down as your MONTHLY NET INCOME. This is commonly referred to as your spendable income. Those who call it thus are correct. This is what you bring home every month to pay bills, put food on the table, keep a roof over your head, and everything else you do in a month. For arguments sake, let's say Don earns $2,000.00 each and every month in exchange for his 50 hours a week, day in and day out. That breaks down to about $10.00 an hour for the time he has given to the job, not counting commuting time nor time spent at home dreading having to go to work the next morning.

Calculate Monthly Net Income

MONTHLY GROSS INCOME	$2,000.00	
WITHHOLDINGS		
SOCIAL SECURITY 6.2%	$ 124.00	
MEDICARE 1.2%	$ 24.00	
INCOME TAX 15%	$ 0.00	
MONTHLY NET INCOME	$1,847.00	

So after willingly giving the government a chunk of his hard earned cash, Don is left with $1,847.00 to spend as he would. First he has to buy survival for his family.

Now make up a column called NECESSITIES. This is where you calculate the FOOD, HOME, and UTILITIES costs. Like I said earlier these three are absolute necessities to survive, unless you like to beg at the local food pantry or live in the homeless shelter. Don't get me wrong, these places are important in society to help those people hurt by circumstances and needing a hand to get back on their feet. But these places are not supposed to be long-term answers to the 3 NECESSITIES.

Let's start with FOOD. Make that a heading under the NECESSITIES column. If you have the receipts for last months grocery shopping, total them up for the entire month. If you don't, then don't worry. Budgets change throughout the first year as you experiment and learn how much money you really need in each category. It has been said by others that 15% of your MONTHLY NET INCOME is what you should allocate for food. I've found that sometimes 15% is not enough money. The actual dollar amount required for you to eat properly and decently will vary according to taste. But be warned, convenience foods and name brand boxed items cost extra.

For a good start to determining a number for your FOOD column, use this formula. As I said before, this is imprecise but will help you guestimate how much money goes into the FOOD category for the month. Once you've kept your receipts for a few months and know just how much you do spend each month than you can adjust your FOOD budget appropriately.

Multiply how many people are in your family by 90 meals a month. Multiply this number by $1. If there are 4 in your family, times 90 meals per person per month times $1 per meal gives you a total of $360. This is what you have to spend for food for the month in your home. This does not count money for eating away from home. That is a separate category and comes later.

Write your number in the column across from FOOD.

At this point I want to stop and say that the percentages I use here are for an average income of between $15,000 and $40,000. It cannot be stressed enough that the lower the family income the larger the percentage that is spent on basic necessities. As such, the HOME category might take 45% of the income instead of the suggested 35%. But please, keep in mind that every budget is individualized to the family and the percentages are guidelines. And guidelines are nothing more than suggestions to help you get started on the road to financial freedom. If you find your budget requires a higher or lower percent than what I suggest take a long hard look at that item. Ask yourself 'Can we find a less expensive way to do this?' and 'Do I really need this?' If you find you must keep the expense where it is, fine. If you can lower it, great and then do so.

Write the word HOME under the NECESSITIES column. Now you can also write sub-categories for your monthly HOME budget. These will include MORTGAGE/RENT (depends of course if you do rent or even if you have a mortgage – there are a few people who own their home outright), INSURANCE, PROPERTY TAX, and MAINTENANCE. These can also be placed under the Discretionary heading, because you can always take the radical approach and not pay any of these, though that is highly not suggested.

A strong rule of thumb touted by Larry Burkett and one that does indeed work out time after time for budgets across the income spectrum is the percentage of your MONTHLY NET INCOME that can go to paying your MORTGAGE. If you spend more than 28% of your MONTHLY NET INCOME on your MORTGAGE you are shorting yourself in another category. Please note, the higher your income, the larger the percentage you COULD spend on your home without really feeling the shortage in another category (up to about 40%).

Write your monthly costs of MORTGAGE/RENT, INSURANCE (liability and personal property), PROPERTY TAX and MAINTENANCE next to the appropriate sub-headings. Now before you get up in arms, I realize that you don't most likely pay your TAX or INSURANCE on a monthly basis. So take your annual payment and divide by twelve. That number is what it is costing you monthly. In the next chapter I will talk about what to do with these numbers so for now write them down and be happy.

These non-MORTGAGE/RENT sub-headings are not supposed to cost you more than 7% of your MONTHLY NET INCOME. Again, if it does cost more than okay, but look to see if you can save costs somewhere by changing insurance carriers, or something. Just remember that if you skimp on the MAINTENANCE it will catch up with you later when you try to sell or when the roof leaks and ruins your carpet. Or worse it could rot out the ceiling supports and you wake up to find the upstairs is now in the downstairs. Not good!

We have covered the HOME itself, your roof over your head. And we've looked at a budget for FOOD – keeping your stomach happy. All that's left in the NECESSITIES category is the UTILITIES.

UTILITIES include electricity, gas (some say heat but I know a few houses are heated and lit by electricity only and thus don't have a separate heating bill), water and sewer. These for a typical $2000 MONTHLY GROSS INCOME family would amount to around 7%. Look at your past utility bills for the year, total them and divide by twelve to calculate your actual twelve month average. I like to use the highest electric bill I had for the budget. This way I will almost always be ready for those more expensive months. Do this with each of the other utility bills as well. The little bit about the monthly average? That was just a little sidebar to show you how much you spend during an average month on each utility.

This is a continuation of the previous charts and examples. The MONTHLY GROSS INCOME is $2,000.00, of which we have already removed $153.00. In this chart we shall remove another 50% just to survive.

Now Don takes out the money for his family to survive – he pays for their food, their house, and their lights. Of course all of this is discretionary, and may be more or less some months.

Calculate Discretionary Money

Monthly Net Income	$1,847.00
FOOD 15%	$ 277.00
HOME 28%	$ 517.00
UTILITIES 7%	$ 129.00
DISCRETIONARY	$ 924.00

A few things about this chart: the percentages are just suggestions and a strong recommendation to limit your spending to that level or lower (if your housing costs less, you can put those funds to work in another portion of your budget), technically, an additional 4% should be added in here to fund the upkeep and mountainous of your HOME, but for practicalities sake and keeping it simple, I shoved that into the DISCRETIONARY portion of the budget.

Oh, and by the way? I do NOT agree that a telephone, television, Internet or other communication device is a necessity under the UTILITIES heading. But more on that later, trust me.

DISCRETIONARY MONEY

You have come through the first half of the budget setting process. You know your MONTHLY GROSS INCOME, your WITHHOLDINGS, and your NECESSITIES. When you remove your WITHHOLDINGS from MONTHLY GROSS INCOME you get your MONTHLY NET INCOME. Subtract NECESSITIES from the MONTHLY NET

INCOME and the dismally small number left over is your DISCRE-TIONARY money.

Remember what I said about your money. If it does not have to go to the government or your necessary expenditures (FOOD, HOME, UTILITIES) than it is DISCRETIONARY. As our good friend Mr. Webster says, DISCRETION is "freedom to act or judge on one's own'. You have the freedom to choose what you will do with the remainder of your monthly income. This includes your automobile, babysitters, going to the dentist, etc. Only thing is, if you mess up, anyone who knows about your mistake will think they have the right to judge you. Tell them to forget it, they're wrong.

I'll give you a quick run down list of what the most common categories and the recommended and suggested percentages of your MONTHLY NET INCOME to allocate on each will be. Let's start.

Category – MAINTENANCE 4%. This is a frequently overlook category of spending. You could always choose not to provide for the upkeep of your HOME, but I am willing to say that in a few years your house will look like a rickety old shack. Remember this old adage – To keep up the value of your home, keep up your home.

Category – TRANSPORTATION 15%. Subheadings include Insurance, Gas & Oil (gotta make it go, you know) Maintenance, Parking (if you must) and Other. The 15% is to cover everything your automobile (or automobiles if you have more) will need to get you from point A to point B. I also include another subheading of Replacement and suggest a mere 5% of your DISCRETIONARY money go towards this. Eventually all cars but go, but the cheapest one you'll ever drive is the one you currently owe nobody for and can keep going. Also – if you live in a low insurance zone you will not need as large of percentage as those who live in say, California.

Category – MEDICAL 5%. Subheadings include Doctor, Dentist, Prescription and Other. What you might use the Other for I'm not sure but I do suggest such a category. If nothing else that money can go towards an unusually large Doctor bill or something. Medical insurance does not come out of this category and as such should be accounted for under the INSURANCE category below.

Category – CLOTHING 5%. Fill in your own subheadings. Work, Play, Kids, Mom, etc. You know you buy clothes and you need to have a budget for it. If you are not the King of the Philippines, how do you propose to pay for 157 pairs of shoes? Control your cash out flow. For every dollar you cut in expenses, you add a dollar to your cash flow margin.

Category – ENTERTAINMENT 5%. I know this isn't much money to fill in all the subheadings such as Eating Out, Babysitter, Vacation, Clubs, and Other. Don't worry though, in the next chapter we can talk a bit about freeing up some cash flow for these very desires.

Category – INSURANCE 5%. Again, this category does not get much money but do not skimp on life insurance if you have small children. I'm not advocating leaving your heirs millionaires, but your spouse should be able to adequately provide for your children. There may be more about this subject later.

Don't forget LIFE, DISABILITY and MEDICAL are the three big insurance costs you will have.

Right now lets look at employer deducted insurance costs. I would like you to notice that your MONTHLY NET INCOME does not include the cost of "benefits" your employer removes every month before you get your paycheck. These "benefits" can include insurance for you and your family, life insurance, other kinds of other insurance and what not. These "benefits" are also DISCRETIONARY as they are not a true necessity to life. So your INSURANCE category expenditures each month will include those your employer removes.

In this case, out of sight IS NOT out of mind. Out of sight is out of control – and if there is one thing that will derail a train on the way to financial freedom it is the loss of control of your money. If you

Another Category you might want to list is GIFTS and these include CHRISTMAS, BIRTHDAY, ANNIVERSARY, as well as Other. If you are giving GIFTS to the tune of more than 2-3% of your income look at the front of this book for my address. Seriously you may want to cut back a bit if you are pinched elsewhere. Giving of gifts is wonderful but like salt or speed, moderate use is wise.

MISCELLANEOUS is a good one to hide those little incidental items under. You know the ones, TOILETRIES, PETS, BEAUTY, HUS-BAND, WIFE, and OTHER. This is the category where you buy the cleaners for the house, and such things that don't neatly fit into another category. This would be well funded at 5% of MONTHLY NET INCOME.

Category – CHILDREN 10%. This category will include ALLOWANCES, SCHOOL LUNCH, TUITION, and of course OTHER. Don't forget to include those instrument lessons every week.

If you tally up the suggested percentages of spending, you will not find an even 100%. This is deliberate because every budget will be different and will reflect the individual needs of the budget maker. However when you are finished with your budget the total percentage must read 100%! If it doesn't you have either under budgeted or over budgeted somewhere. Go back and correct the mistake. While you are at it, go through and double check your allocated funds for each category and sub-heading as well as your math. The fewer mistakes you make the better you will be financially.

Also, you may have noticed that SAVINGS, PAY YOURSELF FIRST and TITHE are not listed. If you could it would be good to put 5% in savings, 10% into your long-range investments, and 10% into charitable giving. However with many people in this economy that kind of spending is neither practicable nor possible. If you can do it even if you only put 1-2% in the SAVINGS and PAY YOURSELF FIRST categories you will come out ahead. I strongly recommend everyone give 10% to charitable causes and you will still find that you are not lacking NECES-SITIES. But who am I to dictate what you do?

I do feel that you need to know the main reason for having a savings account is to be better stewards of your finances. If you have a stash of money you will not need to rely on credit when you have car trouble, a medical emergency, or any other large unexpected event occur for which your budget cannot provide. I advocate maintaining a reserve of cash in savings and in a money market account equivalent to six months of your MONTHLY GROSS INCOME. To build this large of sum of money will take discipline, sacrifice and time – large amounts of time that equal four years or more for the average family. A reserve this large is good for more than just auto emergencies; if you ever loose your job you will be able to live for at least six months while looking for suitable employment.

While we are working away at the figures here, don't forget to include your Financial Goals and Plans in the budget. Most likely your SAVINGS and PAY YOURSELF FIRST will go towards making your dreams come true. Satisfy your NECESSITIES first and then fund your Goals. Don't look at the cutting of money from some of your categories as deprivation but rather think of it as sacrifice to fulfill your Goals. Positive thinking will help a lot when it comes to money.

I don't mean thinking 'I'm positive I don't have enough money'. Get real—even the wealthy think they don't have enough money or else why do they still go to work every day? They have bills just like the rest of us, only theirs are larger.

Oh, gee. What to do with the large amount of money left over? As much as Don would like to, he just cannot fund every category at the rec-ommended level. So he trims a bit here, and tucks some there. Please note this budgetary example is set up as though Don and Dawn are living the 20-80 plan; thus the Tithe and the Pay You categories. Don't worry if you aren't clear what a 20-80 plan is. I'll explain it to you in full detail later in the book.

Sample Budget for Discretionary Money

DISCRETIONARY	$924.00
TITHE 8%	$148.00
PAY YOU 8%	$148.00
AUTO 8%	$148.00
CHILDREN 8%	$148.00
INSURANCE 4%	$ 74.00
MEDICAL 4%	$ 74.00
MAINTENANCE 4%	$ 74.00
CLOTHING 4%	$ 74.00
MISC. 2%	$ 37.00
TOTAL LEFT	$ 0.00

Again, I feel compelled to remind you that this is only a suggested Budget, though a really accurate one. Notice how the numbers have to be juggled a bit to accommodate everything. That's exactly the way you need to tweak your numbers to achieve usage of 100% of your money. You DO NOT want to use more than 100%; that is a severe no-no.

After a few financial date nights have passed, you will be more comfortable with your financial ability and will be able to change the AUTO portion of the budget to more accurately reflect the actual costs of having an auto. Don't forget, when you raise or lower the percentage in one category, some other category needs to have its percentage number raised or lowered as to compensate.

Congratulations are in order once again. Last time it was for the completion of your Financial Plan. By now you have completed your Budget. Yes, I do realize that it might be a bit rough and not at all like you imagined a Budget would look like but get real. You are most likely not a hired financial advisor relying on a smooth and slick presentation for your bread and butter. As long as you know what your spending categories are, how much of your MONTHLY GROSS INCOME you are funding each category with then you have a budget.

Of course, even the federal government has a budget and look how well they stick to it each year. Unfortunately, we don't have the option of printing more money when we run short.

Another parallel to draw from the Federales is that when they work on a budget for the next year it requires many weeks and months and includes much hand wringing, bargaining, threats, and behind the door maneuvering to get a budget ready. Kind of sounds like the dealings a married couple goes through to set up a budget.

You do realize, don't you that even if you have a budget you will not automatically follow it perfectly? I mean, it may take time to get used to the fact that if your eating out money is gone then you stay home and eat. Where's the fun in that? But it is rewarding to see the value of your savings grow and even more importantly, if you did this budget with the aid of your spouse and family then the quarrels about money will occur less often and be less intense. I have been there and done that and life is so much better without the remnants of a financial argument hanging over our heads.

Since you have completed the primary goals of this book, are we done? You've written out a Financial Plan (the roadmap) and completed a Budget (the vehicle to realize the success of your roadmap. Is there anything left to do – YES!!

CHAPTER SIX– PRACTICAL ADVICE FOR IMPLEMENTING A BUDGET

What kind of advice could I possible give you that will help you implement your budget? Well, how about this little tidbit –

- Don't worry if you currently do not have the money on hand to do the budget this month. You are not yet sure just how well you did in deciding how much money to place in the FOOD column, or for TRANSPORTATION or anything. If you start out with absolutely no savings (about 10% of the population) of any kind a reasonable goal will be to be on a solid budget within 12 months.

Outrageous you say? Not really. It will take effort on your part. The fact that you have read this book from the front to this point tells me though that you are willing to work for what you want. So a year of working towards a full budget for your finances is not going to bother you.

FUNDING YOUR BUDGET

The first thing to do if you do not have the money to immediately go onto a budget next month is to cut expenses to the bare bones for one month. Every extra dollar you can scrape together goes into an account you call BUDGET SAVINGS. By the time you have one months worth of MONTHLY NET INCOME, you will most likely already have your budget up and running just fine. Mowing your neighbors lawn and doing odd jobs around town will yield more results than just money – you might meet some new people and don't forget the satisfaction of helping others.

If you get paid every week at your job, set up your monthly expenses so you can pay the bills once a week. Sit down with your spouse at the same time every week and pay the bills due for the week. Not only are you and your spouse accountable to each other for the spending this way, you will have a bit of time together because your children must understand that bill paying time is YOUR TIME. Unless someone is bleeding – then I tell my kids they better interrupt us.

If you have done your budget properly, you will have money left over from your paycheck after paying the bills and taking out the food money. Good for you. Of course, this is not money to go spend on a new toy. Put it into your regular savings account and spend it next week when that really huge electrical bill is due.

As you work at this, you will find you are able to place your weekly income into a savings account until the next week and so only have to pay bills twice a month. You are making your money stretch. Soon your money is stretching for the entire month. Every paycheck goes into a savings account and once a month you are able to remove your MONTHLY NET INCOME from the account and pay your bills and distribute your funds.

IMPLEMENTING MONEY MANAGE-MENT

Now that we have everyone back to a monthly system, let me do a small walk through on the way I have found works very well to control the cash flow. These are just suggestions, feel free to improvise and experiment to see what works best for you. Keeping the goal of financial freedom, managing your money instead of it managing you, following your roadmap of Goals is what this entire budget process is about. Have fun, be young and do well.

REPEAT OF EARLIER INFO

Step one for the walk through is nothing more complicated than getting paid monthly or else having the funds to pay yourself monthly. How do you pay yourself monthly if you get paid weekly? Follow the advice in the paragraph above. Same if you get paid on a bi-weekly system. Put yourself on a budget and stick to it. In a fairly short amount of time you will have enough money saved up to do your bills on a monthly plan.

Oh, one thing I did forget to mention here is that you do not need to save up an entire months worth of income before you start doing your budget on a monthly basis. If you are paid weekly, you only need three weeks saved and if you get your check biweekly then you will only need two weeks income in the bank.

Why?

Because you can combine what is in the bank with what you just brought through the front door and come up with the full months worth of income. Neat, huh?

FINANCIAL DATE NIGHT

Step two is even simpler. All you have to do is pick a day after the last bill has arrived and circle it on your calendar. I've been told that if you want to have a healthy marriage, you and your spouse need time alone so the 'experts' advised having a "date night" once a month.

This bill-paying day you have just circled on your calendar is your financial "date night". Trust me on this one; a 'financial date night' is not as fun as a real date. But it is something you need to do every month like clockwork to keep your finances strong and healthy. Since I am paid on the first of every month I usually pay my bills on the sixth. I say usually because it may get delayed until the seventh but around 9 p.m. on the sixth my spouse and I sit down to pay bills. Any bills that come in the mail after the sixth are saved in a specially designated basket on my desk until the next bill paying time. This method allows you to spread your budgeted funds out once a month and spend (sorry, take) only an hour or less doing so. An added bonus is that you know there will be no nasty surprise bills showing up in the mailbox (and causing all kinds of headaches and arguments about how to pay for that) after you have distributed your money into the allotted categories. Did you ask why? Because you've saved all the bills from the sixth of the previous month and know that they are paid – that's why.

Any bill showing up after the sixth goes into the basket to be paid next month.

DIVIDING THE SPOILS OF WORK

Step three is a bit more complicated. You have your allotment of MONTHLY NET INCOME and are sitting down with your spouse (if you have one) on your financial date night. Now the hard part – What to do with all this money?

Shout 'We're rich, we're rich, we're rich' and throw it in the air. Right? Wrong.

Most likely what you will have is a piece of paper representing your MONTHLY NET INCOME; either as a check or as a receipt for a direct deposit to your bank account. So throwing it in the air will not have the same affect as that much cash in $1 bills.

No, take a clean piece of paper and carefully write down your MONTHLY NET INCOME. Look at the paper containing your budget and examine the categories you have listed and how much you allocated to fund each category. Onto your clean piece of paper, immediately beneath the words MONTHLY NET INCOME transfer your budget categories and amounts. If you want you can subtract after each category or you can wait until the end and subtract the entire works at once.

I'll use the full Budget from our fictitious example couple earlier – Don & Dawn.

Full Budget Sample

Monthly Net Income	$1,847.00
FOOD 15%	$ 277.00
HOME 28%	$ 517.00
UTILITIES 7%	$ 129.00
TITHE 8%	$ 148.00
PAY YOU 8%	$ 148.00
AUTO 8%	$ 148.00
CHILDREN 8%	$ 148.00
INSURANCE 4%	$ 74.00
MEDICAL 4%	$ 74.00
MAINTENANCE 4%	$ 74.00
CLOTHING 4%	$ 74.00
MISC. 2%	$ 37.00
TOTAL LEFT	$ 0.00

Did you end up with a result of $0? If not, go back and look at your budget so you can correct the mistake. Maybe check your math on the once clean piece of paper as well.

Okay, now that you have confirmed that your budget and your MONTHLY NET INCOME equal each other you are ready to move on.

Take another piece of paper and write these categories on it: CASH, HOUSE CHECKING, SAVINGS, and EXPENSE CHECKING. This paper is your TAKE IT TO THE BANK paper. This is what will help keep your banking mistakes to a minimum so everything is distributed properly.

You should have noticed by now that there are two checking accounts listed. HOUSE and EXPENSE. So what gives?

I believe it very advisable to have two checking accounts to easier keep your finances in order. Follow this.

Under the EXPENSE CHECKING write the total of all your bills. I mean telephone, television, Internet, electricity, car payments, the works. If you owe it every month, every quarter, every six months or every year you put the money in this account. Notice I said yearly and quarterly as well. To do this you take your annual bill (like property tax) and divide by twelve and there is your monthly payment. We discussed this earlier in the book, but I know that when something new is learned sometimes something old has to go.

Do not put into this account your monthly FOOD money, GAS money, or anything else. This account is for your must be paid every month type of bills.

Note – this checking account is NOT ever touched for anything other than your regular, reoccurring bills. This is the money needed every month to keep your name clear of overdue charges, delinquency notices, and the stress of wondering how you are going to keep the lights on next month. Hence the name – EXPENSE. It is not the 'I need a new couch' fund or the 'I need this' account.

If you estimate your monthly expenses properly, you will actually have a surplus going into the account every month of at least 5%. Thus if you estimate needing $500 every month for these it would be a great idea for you to be placing $525 a month into the account. A surplus is good for those months when you estimate your long distance telephone bill at $50 and when you open the envelope your jaw hits the floor because it is really $75. Thanks to the surplus in the EXPENSE account, you have the funds available to pay that extra bill without having to dip into SAVINGS. Smart thinking, eh?

On that thought, here's another. Don't forget your life insurance premiums when you put your money into the account. If the premium comes due quarterly, you will have two months when the EXPENSE CHECKING looks real full and you start thinking about taking some of that money out for other things. DON'T!! When the insurance premium bill arrives, that EXPENSE account will be back down in the near depleted area like it should be after your 'financial date night'.

Also, if you do have a really big surplus after one year you should adjust the amount of money you put in the EXPENSE account every month. You are overpaying the EXPENSES. I would always try to have $100 more in the account than you need to pay your bills. A cushion is a very comfortable thing.

Once a year, take any true excess money out of the account and place these funds in the SAVINGS account. Leave the $100 cushion and make sure you are not removing money you will need for a quarterly or annual bill. That kind of action could hurt.

What else, you are asking? Well, how about the reason for both you and your significant other paying the bills together? If just one person takes care of all the bills two things happen. One is that the bill-paying partner feels all the pressure of balancing income and outgo whereas two together can much easier bear the burden. Secondly, both partners know where the family is going financially and how it is doing. There are few surprises.

There are several ways to handle your excess funds from each category. Yes, I am saying you will occasionally have excess funds in a category. Something like Clothing, say. If you budget $48 and only spend $25, keep the $23 difference and add it to next months' $48. There will be times when you have extra one month and the very next month you might not have enough if you did not save the excess.

Oh, one more suggestion.

I highly recommend you live on a 20-80 plan. For those whose income is below about $25,000 net, this plan is very difficult, but not impossible. What a 20-80 plan does is you give away 10% and save 10% of your MONTHLY NET INCOME (hence the 20) and then you pay your NECESSITIES and your DISCRETIONARY spending from the 80%. This method works for most who try it, but it does require you to believe in what you are doing.

So with that said, now is as good of time to review as any.

REVIEW

You will need to have a second checking account labeled EXPENSE ACCOUNT. Into this checking account will go all the money you budget for routine, every month (read monthly payments for those quarterly and annual bills). You will actually be placing a surplus into the account each month of at least 5% more than what you estimate you need for an average month.

On your 'financial date night' you will use this account only to pay your bills. Once a year you can remove any surplus over $100 and place this money in your SAVINGS account.

There we are. In three short steps you have already taken care of one enormous financial burden and in so doing made it possible for you (and your spouse) to breath easier knowing that your EXPENSE account has paid all routine and regular bills.

Take a deep breath, hold it, and exhale. Smile and pat yourself on the back carefully. There is no need to have a medical bill because you broke your arm reaching back to pat yourself.

"But wait!" you say. "What about the other three categories listed on the TAKE IT TO THE BANK paper?"

To which I reply, what about them? They are fairly self-explanatory. Out of the Review mode we drop and back into the new info mode.

How much are you saving this month? $5? Good. Every little bit helps. $500? Even better. You know what a savings account is good for. If you have a big ticket item to buy to achieve one of your financial goals then you can put your money in a savings account to earn interest, keep it a bit farther from your grubby little fingers, and have it protected from loss while you are working to have enough to spend.

Of course, I do have a suggestion. I always do, don't I?

At your local bank have two open and active savings accounts available for your monthly savings. One for your long-term savings – say a year or more. And the second for your short-term savings – that will be anything less than a year. Some items might only take a few months before you have the money. Other things will take longer.

It is up to you to decide how much each month you can put into SAVINGS to use to reach your FINANCIAL GOALS. I suggest as much as you can. But then, I am not in your shoes and thus do not know your situation. But the harder you work for something, the sweeter the reward.

So write down how much you are going to put into SAVINGS this month and into which account. Don't forget that it is not a bad idea to have six months worth of MONTHLY NET INCOME stored away in a good money market account. A money market account would work for your other SAVINGS categories as well, that is up to you.

The HOUSEHOLD CHECKING account gets all the money needed to run the household for the month. Cleaning products, beauty, pet and the like are all things that are bought with funds out of the HOUSEHOLD account. Again, no FOOD, no HUSBAND, and no other such categories are to go through the HOUSEHOLD account. And when the HOUSEHOLD CHECKING is empty, stop writing checks and wait until the next month. This is the best way to control your finances. Quit spending when the book says zero. Deduct all checks when you write them. That way you will not be caught in an overdraft situation and forced to dip into SAVINGS to pay the overdraft, the fee and the penalty.

I've seen a $3 overdrawn check end up costing $35 by the time the bank was through charging penalties and fees and everything else they could dream up. So be careful and know how much is in your account before you write that check.

CASH

Now for that last category heading, your favorite and mine – CASH.

We all love it; it has many uses and comes in a delightful color. But how much cash do we need and why not just drop that wad of dough into a checking account?

The answer is… the cash goes into the envelope system!

What is the envelope system? It goes something like this and believe you me, it is very simple to operate.

Take the money you have allocated for DINING OUT and place it in an envelope in the glove box of your family car. Every time you go and purchase food away from home (no I do not mean food from the grocery store that you will take home), you pay for it with cash from the

DINING OUT envelope. When the money is gone, you have two choices. You either stop eating away from home until the next time you divide up your funds or you take the money from somewhere else.

Realize of course, that if you do take money from some other category – like FUEL – you run the risk of being caught short in that category. It is always best to stop spending when the money is gone. It's not like you are depriving yourself of something you have to have, you are merely having to use what you have available at home.

Other categories under the CASH heading include FUEL (for autos), HUSBAND, WIFE (for personal spending – keep your personal spending away from the HOUSEHOLD CHECKING), FOOD (this is what supplies your house with groceries) and other things. I am vague on this because your CASH needs will be different than mine.

The three envelopes that are carried in the glove box of the family car and never taken out except to spend the money are the FOOD, the FUEL, and the DINING OUT. Never remove these envelopes and carry them with you because just as soon as you do, the money will be spent on something it shouldn't be, or else you will forget to put the envelope back before you need it again.

One more thing about the CASH, it will help you a great deal if you get the biggest denominated bill possible for your CASH categories. If you need $300 for FOOD, get three $100 bills. Same goes for the WIFE and HUSBAND and if you have ALLOWANCE for the children. The bigger the number on the paper money, the more thinking goes into the spending and the wiser you will act when you make a purchase.

So take a few minutes and figure out, on the paper, just how many of each denomination you will need for your CASH categories to be filled.

TAKING IT TO THE BANK

This is what Don's paper would look like as he goes to the bank.

Paper for Bank Transactions

Checking Account		Saving Account	
House	$259.00	Long Term	$150.00
Expense	$1016.00	Short Term	$96.00
Cash $327.00			
1's	II		
5's	I		
10's			
20's	I		
50's	II		
100's	II		

As you look at this, you will notice one small difficulty with this budget. Did you see it? Here's a hint: the only cash is the FOOD money plus $50 taken from the Transportation category to pay for Fuel.

So where's the Dining Out money, the Husband and the Wife money? That is for you to decide. In a simple example like this, I did not want to get to detailed and thus cause confusion.

You will have to remember that anytime you fund one category, the money will not be going to a different category and you must adjust accordingly. Savings (Pay Yourself) is the most common category to be sacrificed.

As another note, Pay Yourself is the method by which you will be funding your Financial Goals. So it is not advisable to cut back on your Savings program if you can trim the money you want (need) from a different portion of your budget.

While we are on the subject of sacrificing our immediate desires for the improvement of our tomorrow—Transportation is a very common category that is not used properly. Too many people will take out the Fuel needs, and maybe a few dollars for a minor repair, but then the rest of the money goes directly into the House Checking Account and spent.

If you can at all train yourself not to do this, go for it. Someday that Auto you are driving will breakdown, or quit completely, and then you will have to go borrow to fix or replace it. Not a very good option if you've had the time to save up a few thousand dollars towards the repair or replacement of your existing auto.

There you have it. Your MONTHLY NET INCOME all neatly reduced down to three columns on your TAKE IT TO THE BANK paper. So what's next? Take it to the bank, of course.

When you go up to the teller, you will have along the slips of paper for depositing into each checking account (if this is your first time you will need to set up the EXPENSE CHECKING), if available have the deposit slip ready for SAVINGS, and remember your TAKE IT TO THE BANK paper. Think how impressed the teller could be when you give her your MONTHLY NET INCOME check and tell her how to divide it. It is likely you will take less than 5 minutes to transact all your business with the bank.

When you walk out of that bank, don't forget to divide out the CASH into the proper envelopes. Once done with that small task, you are set for spending money for another month knowing your bills are paid and you don't have to worry about your finances for another whole month.

Ahhh. What a feeling, right? By the time you walk out of the bank, you most likely will not think about it, but you are extremely glad you picked up this book, followed my advice, and set your financial house in order.

You are off to a great start and are well on your way down the road towards FINANCIAL FREEDOM!!

CHAPTER SEVEN–
SURPLUS? WHAT SURPLUS?

I must have some kind of nerve, talking about a surplus after you just underwent the Budget process. If you are like most people today, you don't have a surplus of any kind except maybe a surplus of shortfalls. That's the kind where you have to cut back in one of your categories to fund another category you just were not willing to trim down any further.

Don't worry, I understand.

THE WINDFALL

No, the surplus I'm talking about right now is in the form of unexpected money. If you find a $20 in the parking lot, or you sell all those aluminum cans you've been collecting in the back shed, even the chance you had a garage sale and cleaned out all the unused, unwanted, and unmanageable clutter in your life (in your house anyway). That money is not money you calculated into your budget because it is a one-time windfall.

Of course, an unexpected inheritance or receiving a sweepstakes prize is also a windfall and so would fit under the general guidelines I'm going to suggest here. After all, a windfall is defined by Webster as 'an unexpected, sudden gain or advantage' – an apt description of a windfall of money, wouldn't you agree?

The very first thing to do is to have already figured out what you are going to do with the windfall. This can easily be done during one of your financial date nights when you are doing a little financial planning. You could call this a SURPLUS PLAN.

Start with asking yourself a few questions…

1.   What percentage are you going to give to charity or church?
2.   Whom are you going to give it to?
3.   What percentage are you going to save?
4.   What are you going to save it for if you do save it?
5.   What percentage are you going to spend?
6.   What are you going to spend it on?

I recognize the fact that if can be difficult to decide what you are going to do with money you don't know the amount of and you don't even have yet. But that is the best time to develop a surplus plan. There are many, many stories out and about regarding sudden money coming to people and within a few short years they are worse off than before they had the money.

Their problem was a lack of a SURPLUS PLAN. So do yourself a favor and sit down and determine what you will do with a surplus.

A SURPLUS PLAN does not need to be complicated. After asking yourself the six questions, write down your answers. It is amazing how much more committed a person and family can be to a plan when it is written out.

Now using numbers I've just pulled out of the air, lets say you have written down that—You will give 10% of any surplus money to the local food pantry. You will save 80% of any found money and place it towards your FINANCIAL GOALS, starting at the top of the list. The remaining 10% you will place into your checkbook and throw away on gifts and whimsical nonsense items. (I do not endorse throwing money away like this, it can lead to a break with the discipline you work for and require to stay on budget and on the highway to Financial Freedom.

Once that is done, determine just how much windfall surplus must you have to follow the SURPLUS PLAN. If you find $2, your actions will likely be different than if you find $20 or if you suddenly receive $200. The easiest and most effective minimum limit for the SUR-PLUS PLAN is $20. After all, how often do you find a $20 bill lying around somewhere? When you do, you act like you found a pot of gold and count that $20 as a significant amount of money. So for your SUR-PLUS PLAN, if you get a surplus of any amount less than $20, just stick in your pocket and call it pocket change.

But when you get $20 or more, then you take it home and apply it in the manner you have determined beforehand. Having a SURPLUS PLAN will save much of the decision making anguish about what to do with the money. The temptation will always be there to go ahead and buy that new_____, or go get a _____. You know the routine. You have been tempted to buy something that looks flashy or has more whistles or just because you like the advertisement. DON'T do it. When windfall money is gone, it's gone.

Before the development of my own SURPLUS PLAN, my wife and I had one windfall of about $5000. We paid a few bills, bought a few items we'd had our eye on for a while and managed to agree on investing 10%. Now, seven years later, can you guess how much that 10% investment has grown into? About $300, is all. The drop in the NASDAQ was very hard on my personal investing portfolio. But then I have never said I am a financial investor. I educate people about finances, not invest for them.

Now that that side bar is done with, can you see what I intend for you to see? If my wife and I'd had a SURPLUS PLAN, we would have given some to those who need help and funded more of our FINANCIAL GOALS. But that is how we learn – from our mistakes. Of course, if you can learn from someone else's mistake you don't have to go through the experience yourself and will thus be able to be further ahead for when you do make a mistake you have to learn from.

OTHER THAN A WINDFALL

Now you're probably saying to yourself 'What about that raise I'm going to get next year? That's certainly not a windfall, I earned that raise'. And you're right. A raise is not a windfall because it is not one time. You keep getting that additional money every paycheck. So here's a good way to handle it.

After tax and tithe take the remainder and apply it towards your FINANCIAL GOALS.

Yes, I know what I am saying. The question is "do you?"

Look at the equation from another angle. You already have your HOUSE fully funded, as are your UTILITIES and your FOOD. The WITHHOLDING is taken before you even see a dime of the additional money, so what else you have to spend it on?

Discretionary spending, that's what. So all I am saying is instead of upping your standard of living by increasing your consumptive spending, why not take that extra $100 a month, share your percentage of tithing, and apply the rest to those GOALS? You will attain them all that much quicker, plus you will not feel guilty when you lay awake in the pre-dawn night thinking about your life.

And on that happy note, I'll wrap up this chapter about surplus. Oh, I guess there is one last thing to talk about.

Don't hoard your money, especially the surplus. Applying a surplus to further your GOALS is one thing, but sticking the entire wad into savings for 'a rainy day' is a not so good idea. You might be hoarding. A few signs of hoarding is saving without a purpose, you sacrifice your family's need so you can accumulate a few more dollars, and your giving slacks off as money takes on more importance than just about anything else.

If you feel the need or the desire, don't hesitate to go back and reread part or even this entire book. Don't forget, this is advice only; I have not set these suggestions in stone saying you have to follow them all. They will act as guidelines for your own financial journey as you work with what you have and know to become Financially Free.

Just remember, money cannot and will never be able to buy happiness. If you remember to be content with how you are doing on the highway of finance, then you have a strong shot at being both happy and successful. If the day comes when you must choose, remember those nine men I talked about at the beginning and choose happiness. Success (defined as money by society) does not guarantee happiness. But happiness can most certainly bring success (as measured by quality) to your life.

After all, it is only money—Your money.

SUGGESTED READING LIST

(I've always wanted to have one of these.)

I suggest you read any and all books that I author in the future about money and finance, as well as any book that catches your eye in the library or the bookstore.

If you get your reading material from the library, your discretionary spending will last longer because you don't have to purchase a library book (of course). Just remember to return it on time!

Remember that anytime you read finance books by different authors, you run the risk of finding contradictory information and suggestions. In that case, you can either flip a coin to see who is right or take their suggestions as just that – suggestions. Then you use the suggestion and information that works for you.

www.ingramcontent.com/pod-product-compliance
Lightning Source LLC
Chambersburg PA
CBHW030900180526
45163CB00004B/1644